JOURNEY FROM INSANITY TO SANITY

A mother's journey with her son

Vicki Chandler

First printing

ISBN 1-58851-172-3
PUBLISHED BY AMERICA HOUSE BOOK PUBLISHERS
www.publishamerica.com
Baltimore

Printed in the United States of America

Dedication

This book is in loving memory of my father. Before my son, my father was my first hero — a man who triumphed against all odds.

Although there are many characters in this story, this is really God's story. It is a testimony of how God provided peace, wisdom, and...people. God used many people in our lives to help us through our trials. It is with overwhelming gratitude that I acknowledge those who played a supportive role in our journey.

I am thankful for the countless friends and family members who faithfully prayed for us, sent cards, shared carefully-selected Bible verses, conveyed their compassion with a hug, and lent a listening ear. I'm grateful for the caring teachers and administrators who supported my son or me. In addition, the staff at my school and our church staff lovingly reached out to us in many ways. Words cannot adequately express the thanks for their contribution to our son's victory.

There are also those who shared in the process of bringing this story of hope to you. My mother edited the book. My aunt, a writer herself, encouraged me to write (decades ago). Last, but not least, my husband helped in countless ways. I am exceedingly thankful for the wonderful relationship our sons have with their father, in spite of all that we've been through.

Preface

Life is uncertain.

At one time or another we will all face uncertainty. It might be the uncertainty of the future regarding marital status or a career. It might be the uncertainty of needs being met (the loss of a home due to fire or natural disaster or the loss of a job). Or it might be the uncertainty of health (your own or that of a loved one). Some uncertainty we experience comes from fears — fears for safety and protection (for those who are alone, or victims of violence or abuse), fears of the unknown, or fears of change. Some people struggle with uncertainty in general; they lack confidence or clear direction in life.

Whether we struggle with uncertainty of the future, our needs being met, our health, from fears, or uncertainty in general, we tend to feel hopeless, helpless and despair. Often we ask, "Why?" or "What caused it?" or "What can I do now?" Even we as a nation ask those questions in the wake of tragedies (shootings at high schools and natural disasters).

Often we continue in our despair because we ask the wrong questions. We should be asking, **"Who?"** Who is able to help us recover, to heal, to protect us in the future? This book answers that question. Although it focuses on one specific tragedy, the feelings and the questions and the answers are the same no matter what your current situation.

Since this is an autobiography, my son and I are the obvious characters in this book. But as you read each chapter, search for the main character — the One who was present in the beginning of my son's life and the One who sustains us today. This is a story about God's love, faithfulness, and provision.

This book is divided into two parts. Each part has a different purpose:

Part One	Part Two
To inspire	To inform
To provide hope	To provide help
To tell a story	To tell some facts

Throughout the story you will read about several conditions: Attention Deficit Hyperactivity Disorder (ADHD), Tourette Syndrome, Post-Traumatic Stress Disorder, Psychosis, Bipolar Disorder, etc. Additional information is provided about each condition in Part Two. Part Two also includes a listing of related support groups and organizations. In addition, several other autobiographies that included family members with mental illness are listed.

This book was intended to speak for and to mothers of children who have a special need — specifically, ADHD and/or mental illness. It should also touch the heart of any person who has a family member who suffers from mental illness. But even if you have never known anyone who suffers from mental illness, hopefully you will learn more about the illness and about the Lord.

It is also my prayer that the Lord will continue His work in my son's life by using his story to bring a greater awareness of mental illness. Left untreated, an individual with mental illness can cause severe pain to many others. But since it is an illness, it often can be treated. In addition, many things can be done to prevent the devastation that can result. Hopefully you will commit to pray for:

- Parents to look to the Lord for wisdom, insight, strength and courage to raise their children
- Less access to guns in our nation
- Health care providers to change their policies as to when individuals can get treatment for mental illness
- Protection for our children in school, and wisdom for school officials and teachers
- Christian teachers and Christian students in our public schools who are trying to point the way to real peace

Only the Lord can bring about true peace in the heart and mind of an individual and a nation.

In closing, you might consider this question: When was the last time you thanked God for your sanity?

The only difference between you and anyone with mental illness is... the grace of God.

Part One

Chapter 1
Preparation for Parenthood

"She's having a psychotic episode," my new supervisor told me.

It was the first day of school and my students were about to arrive any minute. Having been trained for normal blind students, I had taken only one psychology course in college. So I searched my memory for the meaning of "psychotic episode." I was clueless, so I had to admit my ignorance and ask, "What does that mean?"

Mr. Graham told me, "Kim's out of touch with reality." This time I could only ask myself, "What does that mean?" I was trying to comprehend it all and still keep my focus on everything that was about to happen in a typical first day of school with multi-handicapped children. With not an ounce of professionalism, I bluntly asked, "Can I ask a stupid question?...Why is she coming to school?"

He explained to me that her parents wanted her to see the school psychiatrist. Since the psychiatrist wasn't in yet, I would have to deal with her until he did come in. Only 24 years old and a new bride, I had been teaching for only two years. My students were all multi-handicapped. That's why they attended this residential school for the blind.

Little did I know that years later I would come to know first-hand what a psychotic episode is, but on that day it was all new to me. This was not in my lesson plans. What was I supposed to do with her? What was I supposed to do with my other very involved students while I was dealing with her? What was I supposed to tell my aide? I was supposed to be the "expert," and yet it was all new to me. Every teacher prepares thoroughly for the first day of school. Every teacher wants that day to be very special and run very smoothly. Long before school officially begins, many hours are spent to help ease the students' adjustment to their new teacher and new classmates. It is even more important for a special education teacher to be familiar with each student's needs (academic, physical, emotional, social, etc.). I had read all their files. They were all blind, multi-handicapped, and preadolescent. Each one had needs way beyond anything I was trained for.

There was Jim. He was an inner city boy living a turbulent life in addition to his limitations. His father had died a violent death. His mother was an alcoholic. She often had men living with her and she referred to each one as Jim's new father. Being mildly retarded, Jim spoke about each man as though he was his father. I'm sure it was all very confusing to him, especially since he couldn't see each one very well. He probably didn't even know one "father" was different from another. I recall one day when Jim told me he had been locked out of his home by his drunken mother, who was trying to shield him from someone who had been stabbed in their home. It was even confusing to me. It was no surprise Jim's school file looked more like a criminal record. Sometimes he carried a knife to school, he had thrown other (multi-handicapped) students down the steps, and years after I left that school, he tried to burn it down.

Then there was Alice. She, too, was an inner city child. In addition to being blind and mildly retarded, she fantasized. This was different than lying; she truly believed what she was saying to be real. She didn't do it often, so it was hard to determine when she was fantasizing. That wasn't the real problem. The biggest challenge for me was to deal with her in the same class with Jim. It wasn't until months into the year that I found out Alice and Jim didn't like each other. What rocket scientist assigned them to the same class!! Sometimes Alice accused Jim of threatening to attack her with a knife. Trying to ascertain the facts from two students who had limited vision, limited comprehension, significant emotional problems, and significant hate for each other was nearly impossible. And their "witnesses" had similar limitations and difficulties. What a year!

Next was Mary. She had lost just about all her vision in a car accident — the accident that took the lives of both her parents and also left her physically handicapped. Prior to the accident she was mildly mentally retarded. After the accident she was an orphan who was blind, walked with a cane, was mentally retarded and emotionally scarred. She hadn't dealt with her parents' death well. I learned the horror of what can happen emotionally to an individual who doesn't grieve properly. She often spoke of the accident as though it had happened the day before. She would explain the details of the incident as if she were a reporter — relating facts in a cold manner as though it happened to someone else. It was eerie and very difficult to listen to her each time she brought it up.

I had a total of eight students that year, all having numerous needs. Devin was my most involved student. At birth the doctors played God by neglecting to perform a few simple procedures. They saw he had neomylomeningecile (spinal bifida). His backbone wasn't fully formed. In such cases doctors usually put a shunt in the brain to drain excess spinal fluid away. Otherwise, the fluid would cause blindness and mental retardation. Also, they usually fuse the legs so there's a chance the person could someday be able to walk with braces. Neither operation was done. The doctors advised the parents to place Devin in an institution where children like him were warehoused and basically waited to die. It had to have been a living nightmare for those parents to see his handicap, and then to hear those horrifying words of the doctors. But they had other children and were not at all prepared to deal with such a child. They agreed to turn the custody of Devin over to the state. Five years later, against all odds, Devin was still alive. So someone in the system asked the parents if they wanted to take him back. What agony those parents must have felt! How must they have dealt with the guilt of knowing their son had lived in a crippled body without nurturing and love for the first five years of his life? Through their emotion I'm certain they couldn't see clearly the injustice of it all. Surely they would have kept their child when he was first born if they thought he would live. So they did what they thought was the right thing. They took him home. They attempted to deal with his needs, but were ill-equipped.

So after a short time, they relinquished custody of him once again. He returned to an institution that warehoused individuals like him. But this time he knew what it was like to have been part of a family and then rejected. He had experienced the love of his parents and then lost it.

Some teachers have to teach on a limited budget and manage with limited teaching supplies. I've even known teachers who had to begin teaching in the fall without their new textbooks. But I've never known of anyone who had to teach a student who had no working mind. This had not been covered in my teaching methods course in college. All I had to direct me was the Lord. Leaning on the Lord was a new experience for me. Even though I grew up attending church every Sunday, it was all empty religion and tradition. It didn't become real until I was in college and faced a crisis in my life. It wasn't until then that I realized there was a difference between religion and a relationship with the Lord who cares for me personally. I finally realized Jesus died for my sins and that He cares about my life. So all I could do was say a quick prayer and begin my day.

Somehow I managed to welcome my new students and begin to teach with Kim in her catatonic state in the room. After a few hours, the psychiatrist arrived and Kim was taken away. I learned that later that day she was in a fetal position. All I could do for Kim was to pray for her.

In two short weeks Kim returned to school. The psychiatrist told me he had never witnessed such a quick recovery. Although she had been stabilized and was coherent, her healing wasn't complete. The psychiatrist explained to me that she would experience some paranoia. While she wasn't in touch with reality, life went on without her knowledge, so she would think everyone around her was making things up.

As predicted, Kim appeared quite paranoid, confused, and distrustful. Since many of the students at our school exhibited behaviors most people wouldn't understand, visitors had to be approved by the public relations director. Anyone who wanted to tour the buildings had to be approved, and then all of the staff would be notified in advance. My classroom had a window on each side of the door and I kept my door closed while teaching. One time the public relations director neglected to notify us of a tour. Had we been given notice, I would have requested the visitors bypass my classroom so Kim would not be upset. But all of a sudden, without any notice, there were many faces peering into my classroom. Since Kim had enough vision to see to the door, she noticed the faces staring at her. She let out a bone-chilling scream and put her head in her desk. All I could think was "serves them right for not notifying me beforehand!"

The school where I taught was a residential school for students who were visually impaired. Some were day students, but most stayed overnight at the school during the week and went home for the weekends. Getting the job at the school meant I had to move several states away from where I grew up. Until I found a place to live, I was permitted to live in the dorms with the multi-handicapped students. What an experience that was! One student was profoundly retarded and had a mild visual impairment. He was nonverbal and about 16 years old. Physically, he looked just like a 16-year-old; he was very tall and made grunting sounds with a voice that had already changed, indicating he was in puberty. Many students, as involved as he, would stimulate themselves in odd ways. He liked to smell shoes. My bedroom was located near his. The bedroom doors couldn't have locks on them because a student might accidentally lock himself in a room. One night I was awakened to see him walking into my room. He was smiling and walking directly toward me as though he wanted something! Although I was half-asleep, I remained calm. As he approached my bed, he leaned over and picked up my shoes from under my bed. He walked out of my room happily smelling my shoes. The next night I left my shoes at the door for him. Problem solved.

My "next-door neighbor" in that dorm had his own set of problems. Although I never saw him, I heard him all night long. I heard constant banging sounds and heavy thuds. It sounded like someone bouncing off the walls. After my first sleepless night, I asked a staff worker what was going on. She told me he had Attention Deficit Disorder (ADHD) and was given new medication that was having a paradoxical effect; it was making his hyperactivity worse! His parents didn't want him to be seen by the school's physician, so the poor boy had to endure until the weekend so his own physician could prescribe a more appropriate medication. I found out the child was literally bouncing off the walls. He was picking up his metal bed and removing dresser drawers all night.

Those were only two of the many unusual behaviors I was exposed to during the four years while I taught at that school. All of it was fascinating to me. I loved the challenge of finding ways to understand and communicate with them. It was a joy to see even the most involved, non-verbal students blossom when they were treated with respect and dignity. It intrigued me to discover their personalities that were locked behind their behaviors and limitations. I could see that God truly does make us all special and unique no matter what package (body) we come with.

All of my encounters with those students who had emotional problems, mental illness, and ADHD prepared me for parenting. Later, it helped me to draw on the lessons I learned from those experiences.

Chapter 2
"Thank Goodness, He's Normal."

During my fourth year of teaching I became pregnant with our first child. At the end of the school year my husband, Howie, and I moved closer to our parents so our children would grow up near their grandparents and extended family.

When Chris was first born, we were so thankful he was normal and healthy. He was so beautiful. He had lots of hair. So we called him "the luxury model." (Our other son, Robert, was born bald, so we called him our "no frills baby.") Having taught multi-handicapped children, it was fascinating to see a healthy mind at work. It was amazing to watch Chris solve problems at six months old that my mentally retarded teenage students couldn't solve. There were several behaviors that seemed unusual, but as a new mother I simply thought they were just due to Chris's personality. For example, Chris needed very little sleep. No matter what I did, he wouldn't easily fall asleep or stay asleep. I tried letting him cry himself to sleep, but that never worked. I didn't know at that time he had Attention Deficit Hyperactivity Disorder and didn't need the same amount of sleep as most babies. For the same reason, he didn't eat well. He was simply too busy to sit still and eat. He never even nursed for five or ten minutes straight.

When he was only one year old, he did something that really got Howie's and my attention. He had a 15-piece puzzle. Each puzzle piece had a peg attached so it could be held easily, with a separate hole for each piece. The first hole was for the owl piece, so Chris called this his "Owl" puzzle. Whenever he wanted to play with it, he said, "Owl." At 11-months old he could assemble the entire puzzle alone. Howie and I wanted to make it a bit more challenging for him, so we turned all the pieces upside down. Chris instantly assembled the puzzle just as quickly as if they were facing up!! Then Howie covered part of each puzzle piece that was placed upside down, and again Chris assembled the puzzle with ease. Howie and

I looked at each other, finally realizing what Chris could do was extraordinary.

Robert was born when Chris was two. We had been living with my parents for two years and were financially ready to buy our own house. As we looked at the house that seemed just perfect, I mentioned we could put some hooks and eyes on each bedroom door. Since Chris was so active, I knew I had to make some arrangements to keep him safe while I was busy with the baby. The owners of the house seemed shocked to hear we planned on putting locks outside each bedroom. I thought they had just forgotten how active a normal toddler can be.

Once we were in our own home with our two beautiful boys, life was wonderful. God had provided a way for me to stay at home with the boys. I loved not having to work outside the home. I loved being a mother. Life was also interesting. Sometimes Chris did unusual things; for example, he once wrote on his baby brother's bald head! But I hadn't begun to witness some of the things that would happen that would be even more shocking. When Chris was four years old, we knew he wasn't "normal." At the age of four, he could recite long passages of the Bible. It only took one month of nursery school for the headmaster to say he was out of control and they couldn't manage him. Whenever Chris was in a situation with a lot of children or in less-structured situations, he was punished, kicked out, or teased. Every adult we knew had some advice as to how we should raise Chris to improve his behavior (even though we never asked for the advice, nor did any of the adults know Chris as well as we did). This made us feel like inferior, incapable parents. But, in fact, we had to work harder than most parents to be good parents. Thus, we had a psychologist do an evaluation, the results of which revealed his behavior was "out of the normal range" and his IQ was 144!! (very superior). The psychologist recommended we try several things to see if we could get his behavior back into the normal range. He suggested we use time-out, which was not a method we had used since Chris was simply too active. I asked, "What do I do if he doesn't sit still in time-out?" I was told to sit on him! We were also told to try being more consistent. This was all very discouraging and confusing to me, since my supervisors always rated behavior management as my strongest teaching skill! In addition, Howie was a former math teacher, so behavior management wasn't new to either of us. But we agreed to try harder. I asked how long it would take before we would see some improvement. The psychologist told me, "About a year." A year!!! I didn't think I could survive one more day, let alone a year!

A year later we had Chris re-evaluated. The psychologist said his behavior was back in the "normal range," but Howie and I didn't think Chris was okay. We had become more aware of his behavior and believed something was keeping Chris from behaving. His impulsiveness and hyperactivity didn't seem like willful defiance. The most popular parenting book in the Christian community at that time was called The Strong-Willed Child . This book, written by the influential Dr. Dobson, described misbehavior as an act of the will — a result of a strong personality type. But we knew that for Chris, something else was causing him to have difficulty behaving. When I had been a child, my uncle worked for CIBA Pharmaceuticals, who had just developed the drug called Ritalin. It was being administered to children who had Minimal Brain Dysfunction. That was what Attention Deficit Hyperactivity Disorder (ADHD) used to be called. So I had been raised knowing about the disorder. Having been a special education teacher, I knew about hyperactivity from my training and experience. So I had a feeling Chris had ADHD and the psychologist agreed. He said we would find out when Chris started kindergarten. It only took five days before his kindergarten teacher and the principal told me they couldn't handle Chris! I called the pediatrician and told him. Since the pediatrician had all the information the psychologist had gathered, he knew we had tried a full year of interventions. So he willingly prescribed medication. The next day I gave Chris his first dose of Ritalin. I didn't tell his teacher because I didn't want to get feedback from her with the placebo effect. Normally it takes about two weeks before Ritalin reaches its full therapeutic levels in the blood. When I arrived to pick Chris up, his teacher told me whatever I said to Chris worked because he was a different child — a much better-behaved child. I dissolved into tears because I finally knew what was wrong and what was ahead for him. Unlike most parents, I knew exactly what that meant. I knew he would not outgrow ADHD. He would have to work harder to learn certain skills (organization, impulsive control, social skills, study skills, concentration, etc.).

Several years later I attended a workshop for Christian school teachers on the topic of "Helping the Hurting Heart." I learned at that workshop that circumstances initiate the grieving stages, not just the loss of a life. Learning your child has a handicap can cause a parent to grieve. The speaker said finding out your child has some sort of handicap can cause the death of a dream. Life suddenly seems so uncertain and hopeless. When I attended that workshop I reflected back to when I first learned about Chris's ADHD and considered whether I had gone through the stages of grieving. I realized I had indeed experienced shock & denial, anger, bargaining ("If only..."), depression and grief, and then finally acceptance and hope. Since I was quite familiar with ADHD, I didn't remain long in the shock and denial stage. But when Chris was in kindergarten I quickly moved on to the anger stage.

His kindergarten teacher had two quiet, shy, and very proper daughters, so she was not at all tolerant of any active behavior. She literally kept me after school every afternoon to report what Chris had done wrong that day. I'm sure she had no idea how she was humiliating me in front of all the other parents as she repeatedly said, "Oh, Mrs. Chandler, could I speak with you for just a minute?" I was so caught up in my parental emotions, I didn't realize how wrong she was to do that to both me and Chris. Teachers simply don't tell parents every single thing students do wrong every day. They just deal with behavior on their own — that's their job. They only inform parents of major infractions.

In my sorrow I turned to scripture for comfort. I knew God's Word is a living word — that it has something to say about anything. I also knew that all sorts of disabilities were included in the Bible: the blind, the deaf, the lame, the terminally ill (hemophiliacs, lepers), and the mentally retarded (the "simple'"). But I didn't recall reading anything about Attention Deficit Hyperactivity Disorder. So God led me to look for characters in the Bible who seemed to demonstrate all the symptoms of ADHD. I found myself doing a character study of Peter. He surely seemed like a man who had ADHD. He was aggressive (cutting off the ear of one who came to take Jesus away), impulsive (stepping out of a boat and walking on water), and obsessively talkative (speaking at the Mt. of Transfiguration, being the only one at the Passover meal to brag that he would never betray Jesus). Then I considered God's response to Peter. The Lord, who saw beyond his behavior and into his heart, said that on him would He build His church — that Peter would be His rock. That's when I realized the world's view of ADHD is the opposite of God's view. The world views it as a disability, and God views it as a gift that can be used mightily for God's kingdom. The current shift in thinking, even in the world today, is to acknowledge that individuals with ADHD do not have an inability to attend; rather, they have the ability to pay attention to many things at one time.

But years ago I still had to contend with Christians who didn't understand and who added sorrow upon sorrow onto me. One day Chris's kindergarten teacher said she didn't believe Chris had ADHD. I asked her what she thought was causing his behavior, and she said she thought he was emotionally disturbed. For some reason, her opinion devastated me. I suppose it was because she was heartless enough to verbalize what many people thought and wouldn't say. I was also very upset that someone without even a special education degree or a degree in psychology would evaluate my son's behavior as an emotional problem. Who was she to dispute a certified psychologist and a medical doctor? Didn't anyone understand Chris? Couldn't anyone see beyond his behavior? Didn't anyone appreciate his intelligence or the fact that he loved the Lord? That day I realized what it meant to "cry out" to the Lord. I reasoned with the Lord that Howie and I had loved the most difficult students we had. All I asked was that people would realize how special Chris was — how smart he was and how much he loved the Lord. In my helpless, discouraged, and sorrowful state I could see no way for the Lord to answer my plea. With the faith that I used to accept the Lord as my savior, I trusted that the Lord loved Chris and me even though there was no end in sight. I believed the Lord had a perfect plan for Chris's life and I wasn't going to question the path He had chosen. All I wanted was for others to love Chris the same way Howie and I had loved so many others who were difficult to manage. Suddenly I experienced an amazing thing. In the midst of my deepest sorrow, I felt an awesome peace — a peace that passeth understanding. It didn't make any sense that a mother with a broken heart should feel peace, but I did. The greatest agony a mother can experience is to watch her child suffer repeatedly. And the greatest peace anyone can experience is to cast all their cares upon Him and rest in His love (leaving their burdens at the throne knowing God is willing and able to help us when we are brokenhearted). I knew the Lord was in control and He would sustain us in whatever we would have to face. I knew it because of His Word. I knew He was a faithful God and the Bible is full of promises for His children.

The answer to my prayer came swiftly. God made a way for our entire congregation to see just how special Chris was. Each morning I had "breakfast and Bible" with Chris and Robert. We would pray, I would tell a Bible story, and we would memorize verses. Chris was five years old at the time. Chris could recite the old and New Testament passages about the birth of Christ. The one thing Chris loved to do was to run. He loved to run everywhere. He especially loved exploring and running around forbidden places — like near the pulpit at church! One day during the week Chris asked me to take him to church. When I asked him why he wanted to go to church, he told me he wanted to worship at the house of God.

Although I was skeptical, I took him. I fully expected him to run up to the pulpit in the empty church. When he got to the sanctuary, he slowly walked up to the front pew, sat down, bowed his head and began silently praying. After he was finished we went to the church office to visit the secretary. I asked Chris to recite his Christmas verses as a special blessing to her. Once she heard him recite the passage, she called the pastor to hear him. He was so amazed Chris had memorized all that. He asked if Chris would like to recite the verses for the congregation on Christmas Eve. I told him Chris would eagerly agree if he were allowed to stand near the pulpit. A few days later on Christmas Eve I witnessed the powerful hand of God. He had answered the cry of a mother. Overnight Chris had a new reputation in our Christian community.

Since intelligence is valued in our society, many parents want their children to be "gifted." Ironically, I simply wanted a normal child and got a "gifted" son (actually, two gifted sons). It's not easy to raise a child whose IQ is higher than most. Even when his behavior was more manageable, he never really fit in. Once the neighborhood children found out Chris could memorize things easily, they would ask him to perform, rather than simply play with them. At four years of age, Chris could play chess. I recall one day Chris took his chess game outside. He was frustrated because none of the neighborhood children could play chess with him, and none wanted to learn. I told Chris to go in and get another game, so Chris returned with Othello. He didn't understand that most of the children his age wouldn't even want to play checkers. So Robert became his closest friend. Robert was three years old and Chris was five. One day Chris asked me to help Robert play chess with him. I told Chris a three-year-old can't play chess. I said to myself that I didn't know how a four-year-old had learned how to play chess!! After a while Chris called me. He had Robert seated on the floor with a chess board. Proudly Chris told Robert to set up the chess pieces. In shock and amazement I watched my three-year-old correctly set up the board.

When Chris was five years old he enjoyed playing games on our Commodore computer. We had one game called Linking Logic. The goal of the game was to use springs, ladders, and bridges to help a little man get safely from the top of the screen to the bottom. The challenge in logic was to use as few of the springs, ladders, etc. as possible so they could be used for the next level. We had friends visiting one Christmas and I wanted Chris to show our friends his favorite game. As soon as the screen lit up, Chris immediately started moving the joystick to strategically place some ladders and springs along the path. Since Chris had responded so quickly, I assumed he was being impulsive. So I said, "Come on, Chris, take your time and don't fool around so Uncle Bill and Aunt Susan can see how it works."

Howie turned to me and said, "Just watch...he knows what he's doing." To that I responded that I wouldn't be able to solve it that quickly. Howie pointed out that I wasn't Chris. As I watched, Chris swiftly and confidently moved from level to level and won the game. My heart was filled with pride and amazement, and yet it was mixed with concern and sorrow. I thought to myself, "Will we ever be able to challenge him? Can this little hyperactive, bright child ever fit in and be accepted by his peers? Can he ever have a normal life? Will we ever be able to meet all of his special needs?..."

Both boys learned quickly. They were both reading at four. Chris was interested in things like hieroglyphics at five. When we were in the car, Chris would ask me philosophic questions like, "Mommy, when I look at that tree and you look at that tree, do we see the same thing? How do you know we see the same thing?" Both boys learned how to do simple computer programming before they were in second grade. It was hard to establish a normal life for them. I couldn't involve Chris in baseball or soccer because his hyperactivity would cause problems for him. He needed activities that were more structured. So I got the boys involved in gymnastics, bowling, and karate.

At times life was exciting and really fun raising two very precocious boys. Howie was very careful not to exploit them. Their tremendous capacity to remember came in handy, since that was not one of my talents. Also, I could reserve my (limited) brainpower and rely on them to do things like calculate the tip at a restaurant. The real challenge was staying just one step ahead of them, and letting them believe I was smarter than them (which I eventually realized was futile!).

There were many happy times spent with the family when Chris was young. For example, once I started working outside the home, we could afford to go on some vacations. One year we planned to visit Walt Disney World for the first time. Since many of our extended family members had already been there several times, we had a party which included a competition between two teams. We were asked trivia questions about Walt Disney World so when we all went on our vacation, we were expert Disney vacationers! Each summer I was involved with a Christian camp for handicapped children. I was the Assistant Director and the Bible Instructor. It was an overnight camp that lasted only one week and I was able to let our boys attend for free. They had a chance to participate in all the camp activities: instruction (nature, music, Bible, recreation, and art), field trips, skits, and bonfires. It was good for Chris to be exposed to children who had difficulties that were much more limiting than his.

Many of the special needs campers returned every year to the Christian camp. There was one camper, April, who lived with parents who truly knew and loved the Lord. So April had more of an understanding about the Lord and about the Bible than most of the other campers. April always had questions for me that reflected insight and spiritual maturity, so I spent weeks planning Bible lessons in preparation for camp. I'd begin with a weekly theme and then build six lessons around that theme. I had to plan six lessons for each group of campers we had. We usually had a group that was the lowest functioning. They were nonverbal or minimally verbal campers. We also had a group of extremely hyperactive campers. In

23

addition, we had a mildly retarded group, a moderately retarded group, and a learning disabled group.

No matter how much I prepared for the Bible lessons, I was always asked questions I wasn't prepared for. One summer, for example, April told me she mostly had trouble trusting God and wanted me to help her with that problem. How could I help her? Don't we all struggle with that problem? And yet she wanted someone to help her know how to deal with that challenge. I didn't have an answer, but I knew the One who did. If the Lord would give me an answer for her, I knew I could translate it into her simple language. But I only had a few days of camp and I couldn't wait for weeks to get some insight or revelation myself. The Lord was gracious to provide a perfect response to her problem. The next day at Bible instruction I asked April to sit in a wooden chair with arms. I told her I was going to have another counselor slowly tip her chair backwards. I said I would be standing behind her chair and I promised I wouldn't let her fall. As the counselor slowly began to tip her chair backwards, April looked back to check if I was there. As the chair became more tilted, she grabbed tightly onto the arms of the chair. Finally I returned her chair back to its original position. Then we talked about what had just happened. I asked her if she believed I wouldn't let her fall. She said she did believe me. When I asked her why she believed and trusted me, she said, "Because I know you love me." I added that she could trust me because I told her I would not let her fall.

Then I made the comparison. I told her she can trust God because she knows He loves her, He's always there to catch her, and He'll protect her because He said He would. It was interesting to me that she did two things to help herself: she checked to see if I was still behind her, and she grabbed firmly onto the arms of the chair. To me, that was an example of what I sometimes do. At times I feel the need to check and see if God is really there, and sometimes I try to help myself, even though God has promised He would protect me. We both learned a lesson about how we can rest in Him because He loves us, and because His Word is full of promises for us.

Chapter 3
The Elementary Years

Being a mother was the most gratifying occupation and calling for me. Even though it was difficult to manage Chris in group settings, it was very easy for me to manage just him and Robert. I loved taking them to the park, miniature golfing, into the city, to the playground, to watch construction crews, to the zoo, the library, or anyplace where they could move around and be happy together. I also loved doing things with them at home. Sometimes I would get clown make-up and we'd all decorate our faces. We did things like wash the car (and ourselves!!!), blow huge bubbles, cook meals, create with Play Doh, paint, teach our dog tricks, make books, assemble puzzles, play board games, tell stories in the dark, and make forts out of blankets. We all became "Lego maniacs." Often I simply enjoyed watching them play together. Since they were so verbal at such a young age, I loved having "breakfast and Bible" every day.

The medication Chris was taking for his ADHD, Ritalin, was helping him tremendously. The prescription couldn't be renewed over the phone; I had to pick it up at the pediatrician's office and hand-deliver it to the drugstore. Since Ritalin is so highly regulated, I received a monthly lecture from either the pediatrician or the pharmacist. I was never warned of the side effects that could lead to Tourette Syndrome or told how to monitor the drug responsibly. Chris went through a period of twitching his eyes and I thought it was simply a nervous tic. I didn't know at the time that if children are prone to tics and are on a stimulant such as Ritalin, they should be removed from the medication immediately or they can develop the incurable, more stigmatizing Tourette Syndrome. Finally a friend who was a psychologist informed us of the danger and we immediately removed Chris from the medication. At the advice of the psychologist, we took Chris to a neurologist to see if there had been any damage. When I called the pediatrician to inform him of the situation, he yelled at me for not acting sooner because of the potential danger!! The psychologist was able to see clearly through his reaction. He explained that the pediatrician was coming on strong because he knew he hadn't informed me of the dangers. Later the pediatrician suggested I take Chris to see a neurologist. I told him I had already done that, so he asked me what the neurologist had said. I told him the neurologist basically said all the same things he had told me on the phone, but in a much nicer way. To that the pediatrician said, "Mrs. Chandler, I know it's hard to have a child with ADHD." Now that I was much more calm and prepared, I chastised him for the way he treated me and explained that there is no way for him to know what it's like to live with a child who has ADHD. I went on to tell him he should never speak to a mother like that again. I instructed him to give out the booklets I had purchased and brought for parents of ADHD children, and told him to have parents call me if they needed to talk to someone who would understand.

That same pediatrician prescribed Toffranil, another brand name stimulant for Chris. Being desperate, I was thankful there was an option. Later at a symposium I attended on ADD, I learned that children who are prone to tics should never be given any stimulants (regardless of the brand name); otherwise they could develop Tourrette Syndrome. That statement seemed so logical to me, but I didn't want to believe it because Chris had been on another stimulant for quite a while. I soon learned that Chris's sniffing and coughing, which I thought were cold symptoms, were actually tics. Around that time we visited Gettysburg, Pennsylvania and I noticed a headquarters for Tourrette Syndrome. When I read the literature I obtained from that office, I learned there are degrees of Tourrette Syndrome; someone can have the syndrome without the commonly known symptoms (e. g., calling out curses). I realized Chris had exhibited at least 90% of the tics for mild Tourrette Syndrome. I didn't take him to the doctor to get him officially diagnosed with Tourrette Syndrome because I knew there really wasn't any cure for it. Since Chris was able to control or substitute his tics, I saw no need to put him on any medication or start biofeedback therapy (to control his tics).

As Chris was entering first grade, we wanted him to continue attending Christian school, but on one salary it was hard to swing financially. So, it was time for me to go back to teaching. When I went to college I had to have a double major in order to get a degree in special education. I also had to be certified to teach regular elementary education. I never intended to use that training, but the Lord knew I would need it. With that training, I was able to get a job at a local Christian school that waived the boys' tuition if I taught there. I was hired to teach second grade at Mercy Christian School (MCS), a small school affiliated with a Baptist church.

At MCS there were some very talented and gifted teachers, and some...who were not. Robert's kindergarten teacher wasn't quite prepared for a five-year-old who could read. It was Robert's routine to read himself to sleep at naptime. At parent-teacher conference time, his teacher told me he was disrupting the others at naptime. This was hard for me to hear, since that is the kind of thing I always heard about Chris, but never Robert. When I explained his routine at home (of reading himself to sleep), she said he had asked to read books at naptime, but she could not allow that. When I asked why that was so, she explained if she let him read, all the other students would want to read and they were not yet able. A few years later that teacher got her masters in reading and became a reading teacher!

Chris's first grade teacher was wonderful. She knew when to "pick her battles" with Chris, and she celebrated his inquisitive mind. Chris's problems at that school were mostly with other students who sensed how vulnerable he was. They could taunt him without being caught by the teachers, and watch him retaliate and get in trouble (because he didn't pay attention to whether the teacher was looking or not). Since the other students who bullied Chris were not caught, their maliciousness toward Chris became more blatant. Years later as I stood in Chris's class talking to his teacher, Joe came up to Chris and punched him in the stomach totally unprovoked (right in front of his teacher and in front of me!!!). It was all I could do to keep from strangling him, but I resisted and waited for his teacher to deal with it. To my shock, she said and did nothing!! Another incident that is a scar on my heart was when Chris was held down by several students at recess so Joe could kick and hit Chris unmercifully. With numerous student witnesses and several teachers reporting that Chris didn't do anything to provoke such behavior or even fight back, the Principal did nothing!!! Joe was never punished.

My problems at that school were mostly with administrators who were not at all equipped to deal with a child with ADHD. Little was known about ADHD at the time. It's hard to believe now that when I called a local hospital to find out when the Children with Attention Deficit Disorders (CHADD) meetings were, they told me the meetings had been discontinued due to lack of attendance. Nowadays, it seems that CHADD is a household name. The Principal at the school didn't know how to handle Chris except to punish him. All that punishment accomplished was to reinforce for Chris that something was wrong with him and he deserved to be rejected everywhere he went. All of the punishment succeeded in damaging my spirit. I've since been able to come to some acceptance of the whole situation. I choose to believe the Principal (and even the Pastor of the church affiliated with that school) never intended to hurt Chris and me as badly as they did; they were just ignorant and ill-equipped to deal with a child with ADHD. They thought it was kind to keep him in their school, when the most loving thing would have been to admit they were not able to help Chris gain the skills he needed to learn.

When Chris was in fifth grade, the Lord made it clear we should put him in public school. Chris had a first-year teacher who was not able to effectively manage her class, let alone a student with ADHD. Many parents know how hard it is to let one of their children experience all the mistakes first-year teachers must make. It's even harder when one of your children has difficulties with behavior, attention, study skills, and organization. It's even worse when that one child needs to be challenged academically, and it's intolerable when the mother of that child has to share a wall with that teacher!!! With my classroom situated next door to Chris's fifth grade teacher, I had to listen to her all day. I could hear her publicly ridicule my son as she repeatedly singled him out. I often wondered how she could even hear his voice among the chaos of all her students who equally disrupted my class!

Chris became the scapegoat for everything. He often got blamed unfairly, or when he was at fault he was the only one in trouble. Things became very hard for Chris, and he couldn't take it any more. It was unbearable to deal with students who taunted and hurt him, a teacher who was unfair, and a Principal who didn't protect him. So one day he simply left school and hid. He was missing, but no one had the courage to let me know. It wasn't until they found him that they told me what had happened. Realizing Chris needed some form of relief during his day, I made him promise if he needed to run away again, he would go and hide in an agreed-upon place within the building. He agreed to hide in the bathroom high up on a ledge. Soon after the first incident, Chris was missing again. This time they informed me and I found him just where he promised to be. I was thankful God had given me the wisdom to know how to help my son, and the insight to see his extreme pain and feelings of helplessness.

God was gracious one day to let me see a part of His plan for allowing Chris to go through so much. Chris offered to take the punishment of one of my students at recess. Chris didn't even know the student. All he knew was there was a boy who had to miss recess and Chris offered to take his punishment for him. I found out when my student told me what Chris had offered to do. It became evident to me that Chris had a sensitivity to others who struggled with behavior, and his heart went out to them. I could see that God would one day use the character He was building in my son through his painful experiences.

By the age of 10, Chris had received enough punishments and consequences for a lifetime. It was frustrating for me, since I knew what he needed and somehow couldn't convince some of his teachers and administrators to provide an appropriate education for him. Often parents and teachers continue doing what they know doesn't work, using only punishment and rewards (which oftentimes are actually bribes when given before the desired behaviors). Behavior is a procedure that must be practiced properly to be mastered. No one would teach a teenager to drive a car simply by sitting down and explaining it to them. If the teen had an accident, it would seem ridiculous to sit him down again and review how to drive a car correctly. The best way to learn a procedure such as driving a car and behaving correctly is to practice it. Chris needed to be taught how to manage his behavior. He needed to be given opportunities to do things the right way. The Bible teaches us to train our children. I believe the Bible is the best guide to parenting and behavior management. In it there are examples of:

- Behavior modification (surely God rewards those who asked to be saved and who live their lives according to His will)
- Time out (Jonah was put in one huge time-out place!)
- Reasoning
- Teaching by example (Christ was sent to the Earth not only to die for our sins, but to be an example of how we should live)
- Repeated instructions, reworded instructions, and warnings (God, Himself gave us His Ten Commandments and then Jesus summarized the law into two simple commands: love God and love others)
- Structuring the environment to set up for success (even the Lord taught us to ask God not to lead us into temptation)
- Logical consequences (Lot's wife was warned not to turn around lest she be turned into a pillar of salt, and often God gives us over to our sin)
- Punishment

The Bible also includes many examples of when God extended mercy towards individuals who were repentant. It is clear that God deals with us as individuals. In the case of a child with ADHD, parents and teachers need to teach the skills the children don't otherwise learn incidentally. Chris's fourth-grade teacher knew exactly how to train Chris. That year he didn't need medication.

When Chris was in fifth grade we took him to a Christian psychologist to help him deal with all the injustices of life. Surely he was out of control, aggressive, and impulsive. Dr. Kipley explained to Chris, to my husband, and to me that Chris needed to find his specialness in what God did for him — that the God of the universe sent His Son to die for Chris, and that God created him perfectly with a perfect plan for his life. Dr. Kipley also instructed us to make home a safe haven for Chris.

Making home a safe haven was extremely difficult for me. It took a great deal of energy to minister to my son's broken emotions from the day. After teaching 26 second graders all day, I came home and spent up to an hour listening to Chris. I validated his crushed feelings without allowing him to harbor bitterness or anger. I never let him use his ADHD as an excuse to get away with inappropriate behavior. I vowed to help Chris with the skills he needed to learn and to help structure his environment so he could meet with success. I never let him have a "pity party." I pointed out to him that, although it seemed unfair that he suffered all his difficulties because he was born with ADHD, many other children suffer far worse in life: some children need to have operations all their lives, some are born into poverty, some are born in war-torn countries, and some are orphans and never know the love of a parent. I lovingly would share God's Word with him, letting him know that God knows his heart and his pain. I shared all the promises God's Word has for His children. We would pray specifically about certain problems, asking the Lord to stop all those who would seek to torment him. Then we would pray for Chris's enemies, and for wisdom for the teachers and Principal.

Sometimes God answered those prayers in a way that would seem contradictory to our ways. When Chris was feeling the worst, it was then God would allow someone to hurt him unmercifully (physically or emotionally). But then many students and teachers would rally around him to defend him and to show how they cared about him. So, we learned that God's ways really aren't like our ways, but God's ways always are for good.

It was difficult for Chris to deal with his intelligence, at times — rather, it was difficult for his teachers to deal with his intelligence at times. Since math was Chris's greatest strength, he could instantly get the correct answers to the problems assigned to him. He never could understand why he had to "show the work." Showing his work seemed so tedious and unnecessary to him. That just added to his frustration. Being a teacher myself, I tried to help him understand that he couldn't be given the special privilege of not showing his work. Then other students would want that same privilege and the other students probably couldn't solve the problems in their heads without using a calculator. When Chris was in second grade, I was his teacher. Even I added to his frustration. I remember one night I was grading creative writing papers. Trying to decipher a stack of papers written by seven-year-olds is quite draining. Their "inventive spelling" often left no hint of the word that was being attempted. Finally I got to Chris's story. As I read his lengthy story, it made no sense to me. There was no clear story line; thoughts seemed to jump around. In my frustration, I called him over to me and began to reprimand him. I told him to take it back and start over. He glanced at it and casually said, "Oh, I see the problem." After a few brief moments he handed back the papers to me. He had added numbers to each paper heading. He also added words at the bottom of each page. Essentially, he had created a "Choose-Your-Own-Adventure" story. With the pages numbered and the notes on the bottom of each page, it was obvious he had written a perfectly brilliant story. My heart ached because I had added to his mistreatment based on my misunderstanding of him. But I've learned to forgive myself (and others) who meant no harm.

Dr. Kipley, Chris's Christian psychologist, had recommended we put Chris into public school since they were more knowledgeable about his needs. But we lived in a big city and wouldn't consider putting him into the city schools. I remembered having arranged to have Chris participate in the "gifted" program one day a week at the local public school so he would have something positive in his life in an environment where he would be understood. Chris joined the program in October, so he was the only new student (in a class of less than 10 students). Chris preferred the discovery approach to learning. Often he would race Howie and me to try to figure out directions to some new computer software. He would use his discovery approach and we would read the directions. Usually Chris would beat us or we'd figure it out at the same time. On that first day in his "gifted" class, Chris wanted to learn something his way and the teacher wanted him to follow her directions. Since Chris wasn't fully paying attention to the teacher, she yelled at him in front of his new classmates. Later that day Chris begged me not to take him back to that class, adding that he would rather die than go to that class! (he was only in fourth grade at the time). So Howie and I simply called the public school to say Chris wouldn't be returning to that class. We didn't even make an issue of the way the teacher handled him. We received a phone call from the teacher asking us why we pulled him out of the program. After explaining our reason, she admitted dealing with him in that manner, but didn't think it would bother him. With all the self-control I could muster from the Lord, I explained that any ADULT wouldn't want to be ridiculed in front of their peers the first day on a job. I also added that teachers who have many more students than she often find a way to privately correct their students. All school districts have their fair share of good and bad teachers, but some districts are better than others. It was common opinion (even among their own teachers) that our city public school district left much to be desired, to say the least. If we wanted our boys to attend public school, it would have to be a suburban district and we would have to move.

In order for us to afford a house in the suburbs, I would have to get a teaching job in a suburban district. The competition for jobs in the suburban districts was tough. One year a suburban district had 14,000 teaching applications for only 70 positions. Most people secured a teaching position after first substituting for several years or after taking a teaching assistant's position. So I had to make myself more marketable. During the time the boys attended MCS, I spent three years attending graduate school to get my master's in special education. I never aspired to be a career woman; I simply did whatever it took to be the best mother I could be for Chris and Robert.

When Chris was having his terrible year in fifth grade, I was finishing up my master's degree. During the spring I had to take two courses, in addition to teaching and ministering to Chris, as well as prepare the house for a move (in the event I got a job in the suburbs). I was also filling out teacher applications to about 27 local school districts (each requiring an essay equivalent to a term paper in college). If I didn't get a teaching position, I planned on home schooling the boys.

It was around that time that my father was struggling with cancer. By the summer, things didn't look promising. The radiation treatments near his throat had destroyed his taste buds, so food tasted like cardboard to him. Since it was so difficult for him to swallow, he had a feeding tube inserted in his stomach. My sister was just going through a divorce. All summer I went to interviews. I was thankful I was even called for an interview, since most candidates never reached that point in the application process. Going to interviews was like an emotional roller coaster. I'd get excited and hopeful when I was called for an interview, and then I'd be devastated and frustrated when I was turned down for a position, wondering why God allowed me to go through it all.

It wasn't until the last week of August that I got a job. I had one week to find a place to live; pack up our house; find a real estate agent; get medical records and select a school district for the boys; buy a new car (because I was hired as an itinerant vision teacher); and attend an in-service for my new job. I took the boys to my mother's house an hour away for her to take care of them. During that week Robert broke his arm. As I listened to his shaky whimpers on the phone begging me to come to him, I knew there was no way for me to leave; it was impossible for me to do all I needed to do even in one week. I had to ignore the maternal emotions just below the surface and assure him his grandmother would take care of him just fine and that he'd be okay.

I found a nice townhouse development located in an excellent school district near my work and close to a train station for Howie. Now that we finally were away from MCS and living in the suburbs, I thought everything would be fine. It's a blessing we don't know the future.

Chapter 4
A New Level Of Trusting God (Middle School)

Since I was familiar with the recent research on ADHD (in 1986), I was aware of the fact that, although individuals don't ever outgrow ADHD, people learn to manage their hyperactivity when they reach adolescence. So, unlike most parents, I was looking forward to less stress during Chris's teenage years. Sadly, that would not be the case. Most people still didn't know much about ADHD and there was still a lack of tolerance for the behaviors of students with ADHD. There were few training programs for educators (even in the field of special education) to properly prepare them to teach the skills a child with ADHD needs to learn. As Chris's mother, I continued to be an advocate, coach, counselor, and trainer. As he encountered more difficulties at school, I learned that God's ways truly are amazing. He uses everything for good (our talents, successes, weaknesses, and trials). We don't always know why God allows certain things to come into our lives. In my case, however, God was gracious enough to show me how He would use what I was going through with Chris. I began to see that I was becoming a better teacher. I could have more compassion with students with ADHD and other special needs. I was better equipped to train them. I was also able to be more empathetic with their parents. I could speak the words of healing I wished teachers had spoken to me. I acknowledged that they face many relatives, friends, neighbors, and strangers who think they are failures as parents. I could tell them I know the truth is that they are working harder than most parents ever will. I compliment them for their perseverance, effort, continued love, and commitment to their children who are difficult to manage. Parents of my ADHD students couldn't say to me, "You don't know what it's like." Whenever I asked them to do something to help their children, I knew what I was asking was realistic and possible — with God's help. I had been there, done that.

The townhouse I had selected didn't allow pets. I informed the boys we would have to get rid of our Cocker Spaniel, Zelda (named after a Nintendo program!) because we couldn't afford to board her somewhere. Robert (9 years old at the time) burst into tears and Chris, who was 11 years old said, "I'll get a job." It was final...we would find a place to board Zelda (and, no, Chris did not get a job to pay for it, we paid for it). A friend of my cousin had a friend who lived in a rural area very far away who would be willing to board Zelda for a very reasonable cost. She knew we probably wouldn't be able to take Zelda back to live with us until we moved into a home (which probably would be about nine months away, after the school year). The lady who boarded Zelda was very kind to let Zelda live in their home during those long months. Otherwise Zelda would have gotten "kennel brain" from being kept there for so long. Periodically, we would call just to see how she was doing. We told people our dog was in "foster care."

When Chris got home from his first day at his new school, I asked him what his impressions were. He said his new school looked like "a mall!" Compared to the tiny little Christian school he had attended for so long, I suppose his new school did look like a mall to him. It was huge.

At first, when Chris was in sixth grade, it was hard to remember it was God's will for him to be in public school. We had hoped all his problems would be over, but there he was, publicly ridiculed by one of his teachers. After only a few days of school, the teacher held up one student's paper and said, "This student will pass sixth grade with this kind of work." Then she held up Chris's paper and announced that he probably wouldn't pass sixth grade. How devastating that must have been for a teenager who was new, expecting to be treated better in this place, and who knew he could probably complete the work for seventh grade! When Chris shared that story with me, I knew it would be time for me to, once again, comfort, affirm, and teach him how Christians respond to that sort of thing (to forgive, with God's help). At that time I chose not to approach the teacher. Often parents are worried that doing so might make things more difficult for their child. I prayed for the emotional strength to go on, and to have the wisdom to know which battles to pick.

Soon it became clear I had a "battle to pick" with that teacher. Chris said the same teacher told him to sit in a beanbag chair near her locker in the classroom. While sitting in that chair, Chris locked the lock on her locker. For that, the teacher publicly reprimanded him, saying he should be in special ed. It was time to ask for a meeting with the teacher, the Principal, and Howie and me. It shocked me to hear the teacher casually admit in front of the Principal that she had made that comment. She added that she really didn't think it would bother him. I informed her she probably had inflicted an emotional scar that would remain for his lifetime. The teacher received no consequences. Chris had to stay in her class for the remainder of the year.

Each day when Chris would come home on the bus from sixth grade, one of the other students would follow him and sometimes annoy him. He would tease Chris, and one day he had some friends hold him while he punched him. The school told me they could not do anything about it because it was happening after they got off the bus. The police said if they got involved, the situation could get worse for Chris. So every day as I came home from work I would check him to see how he was doing physically and emotionally. Later, I would learn Chris (and I) was experiencing a real trauma because of that troubled stalker and bully.

In the midst of all the adjustments and frustrations Chris had to face, he still was able to hold it all together. Since he was a "latch-key kid," I couldn't be home with him when he returned from school. He had to begin his homework on his own. Attending to homework is not easy for a child with ADHD, even when supervised by an adult, but somehow Chris was able to discipline himself and focus. When I arrived home each day, I usually would find Chris watching TV or playing Nintendo. When I'd asked him if he had started his homework, he'd respond by saying he was "taking a break." I thought to myself, "Yea, I'll bet!... He's probably been on a break since he's been home!" But I couldn't bring myself to add more pressures to his life. So, I told him I would trust him to take care of getting his homework done unless I found out his "system" wasn't working. Amazingly, when he got his first report card he received all A's and B's (except for a C from the lady who thought he should be in special education!).

During that school year I experienced numerous trials and difficulties. My father died of cancer. We were being stretched financially as we paid for the mortgage on our house (that we didn't sell yet), the rent for our townhouse, boarding Zelda, payments for a new car, etc. Then I found out my job (teaching visually impaired students) was extremely unstable; any day I could be laid off. So I had to continue looking for more permanent teaching positions and going to interviews (which wasn't easy to manage while I was working!). I was informed there was the probability I would have to face two hearings regarding two of my students. The parents of one of my students had hired one of the best lawyers in the state to oppose the school district. We had several highly stressful meetings regarding just that one student. In addition to doing lesson plans, I had to do a great deal of Braille each night. Things weren't going well between Howie and me either. As an itinerant teacher, I traveled around to ten different schools every week. To complicate my life even more, I broke my toe one day. I began to think the Lord had put a sign on my back that read, "Kick me hard!"

Even while my father was dying of cancer and my sister was going through a divorce, my mother found ways to help me. She paid for karate lessons for Chris and Robert. Now that I look back, I can't remember how one day seemed worse than another. I do remember, however, that one day I was feeling extremely frustrated and discouraged. My mother drove an hour and a half to be with me that day.

During the school year we sold our house and in June were able to move into a new home. We chose to live in another school district. I've met many parents who cannot handle change themselves, let alone help their children adjust to a change in schools. But Howie and I presented this second move to the boys as an opportunity to start all over again. Many people fear the unknown and so they resist change. But we, as Christians, can trust the God of the future to guide us through the changes we all must and will face. Therefore, we weren't fearful of the adjustments we would have to make. Besides, what could happen that we hadn't already faced?

When the fall came, Chris and Robert went to their new schools and I started a new job (one with more stability). In seventh and eighth grades Chris encountered more tormenting. Other students frequently knocked his books out of his arms in the hallways. When Howie spoke with the vice principal about it, he was told many of the students have to deal with that (it was a common problem). Implied in his response was the message that we shouldn't worry about it because Chris wasn't the only one being mistreated in that way and so it was no big deal (certainly not one that was going to be stopped by the administration!).

Often Chris would come home with small bruises on his legs. Once we questioned him about it. Apparently they were injuries he sustained from being bombarded with coins in the gym locker room. It wasn't until years later that we discovered he had suffered other traumas: someone had put a knife to his throat and threatened him, and some other students locked him inside a locker.

Those were the years Chris won several academic competitions (in math and in chess). Another indication of Chris's extraordinary drive and motivation was that he asked to go off his medication for his ADHD. He continued taking karate lessons. He started bowling and began playing the saxophone.

Having completed my masters program at graduate school, I found time to read many of the books written by Barbara Johnson (a modern day Job). In one of her books she described a "joy box" that she had. She collected things that would make her laugh, knowing that "A joyful heart is good medicine..." (Proverbs 17:22). That was one way she dealt with the incredible losses she had experienced in her life. She inspired me to develop my own "joy box" as a way of using humor to heal my hurting heart.

My role during those years was to help Chris through prayer and faith in God. With a more demanding job, I couldn't be as directly involved with Chris as I had been in the past (nor should I — as Chris reached adolescence he wanted to be more responsible for his needs).

Chapter 5
Out of the Valley? (Early High School)

Things appeared to be much better when Chris was in ninth and tenth grades. He joined the marching band, started bowling, earned his black belt in karate, and seemed much happier. Chris was earning all A's and B's in school. He remained in his room quite a bit. We assumed he was studying, reading, and playing with his Super Nintendo.

Life was getting busier. The boys were more involved in extracurricular activities. Work was getting more challenging for me. I had to spend longer hours at school, and work harder on school work at night. Then the Lord led me to begin a support group for parents of special needs children. Believe me, it was not my idea! One day I was listening to Christian radio. A mother of a child with ADHD was sharing how the Lord was working in her life. During that broadcast, the mother spoke about how she felt so lonely, like no one (even in the church) understood what she was going through. As I listened, I answered to Myself. "I know what that's like!" Since I was attending a church with about 6,000 members and growing strong, there must be other parents with ADHD children who also feel alone. I knew how exhausting it is to survive life with a child so difficult to manage and raise. And yet, I felt stronger and more confident than ever. I had experienced many trials and had survived with God's help. I knew I could facilitate a support group for parents, but I was busy with my own life. Besides, I was finally enjoying an uncomplicated existence. I rationalized that the pastors of our church rarely approve such ministries because too many people want to start one for the wrong reasons (being led by pride rather than by the Lord).

When I arrived home, I got a phone call from our senior pastor's wife. I didn't mention what the Lord was nudging me to do. I rationalized that it was sheer coincidence she had called me that very day. But when she called again the next day, I was out of excuses for the Lord. So I mentioned the idea to her, downplaying it as much as possible (so I could tell the Lord that, well, at least I had tried!). Our pastor's wife thought it was a wonderful idea. She added that she was sure her husband would approve of me starting such a group because at least I was normal (and not someone who would go off on some strange direction while leading discussions). I told her I tried very hard not to be normal. Being normal is overrated in our society. Most of my favorite people (big and little) are not normal. Normal people tend to be quite boring and predictable, uncreative, and sometimes prideful. Give me someone who is abnormal any day! I once had a conversation with a teenage camper who had Down Syndrome. She was raised Catholic. Every time one of her parents' Catholic friends met her they would say the common Catholic expression, "Oh, that's a sin" (that she's mentally retarded). Being a concrete learner, the girl literally thought it was a sin to be mentally retarded. She thought she wouldn't go to heaven. She asked me if heaven would have mentally retarded children there. I assured her that Jesus died for mentally retarded children. I told her that Jesus even said that we all must become like little children who have child-like faith. Since mentally retarded children have child-like faith, then we should all try to be like them when it comes to spiritual matters. I ended that little discussion by saying I hoped God was preparing my mansion in heaven so people who lived in handicapped bodies while on earth would surround me.

In 1991 I got a teaching job where I worked with a team of educators to help teachers solve problems students face in the regular classrooms (academic, behavior, or study-skill problems). My position was kind of like a lead teacher. I had to collect data by doing assessments and formal classroom observations. Teachers with this position had to have several areas of certification and many years of teaching experience. My paperwork changed from grading papers to writing reports. Instead of having a classroom of only a few challenging students, I had a caseload of challenges. Parents and teachers looked to me to help them properly identify problems and to help find strategies so that their struggling students could succeed. It was quite challenging. I no longer had any time to catch a quick nap when I got home from work. So I started to eat foods high in carbohydrates so I could take care of my responsibilities at home in the evening.

Without even trying, I kept getting calls for interviews for jobs in other school districts. I pursued the interviews just in case this was the Lord at work. I didn't look forward to changing jobs for a third year in a row, but I wasn't so foolish as to argue with God's leading either. I was offered a position in a school district that had an excellent reputation (of being the finest in the area) and which paid extremely well. I accepted it and found myself teaching fifth and sixth grade students who were in special education primarily because of their behaviors (either aggressive or oppositional). I was trained and certified in non-aversive holds.

Less than a year later, our church was making plans to start a new school. Years before I had taught our senior pastor's two older children when they were in second grade. At that time he said he had dreams of starting a Christian school for the children of the parents of our congregation. He spoke to me about how he'd like to have special education in that school and he would want me to teach in it. I didn't really believe it would ever become a reality, but I smiled and said, "That would be wonderful." With a new building just completed, they were moving ahead with the plans; it was going to become a reality. My pastor asked me to work at the school. It was my dream come true, but I had worked hard to get a job in the suburbs so Chris could attend a school in a good district. For so long I had gotten used to the idea that the Lord wanted me to teach in the public schools. So I didn't jump at the chance because I was confused. I wanted to pray about it and talk to Howie to decide if it was God's will for me to change jobs again.

Since I was making a good salary, I didn't expect Howie to agree for me to take a substantial cut in pay and switch to the new Christian school. But surprisingly, without a great deal of agonizing over the decision, Howie told me to accept the position offered by our pastor. I hadn't even begun to get used to the idea, and wasn't sure it was the Lord's will. But I figured if Howie felt it was the right thing to do, it must be the Lord's will.

When I let my pastor know I would teach at the school the next year, he said he actually wanted me to be an administrator. Well, that was the farthest thing from my mind as a career option! My own brother had gotten his doctorate degree from Harvard in education administration and I personally thought administration was a waste of a good education. My sister was also an administrator in a facility for mentally retarded adults. I know she, like many administrators, was feeling burnt out. Reluctantly, I sought the Lord's will on the matter. After spending a weekend in prayer and in God's Word, it became apparent I was doomed to be an administrator. Even though I knew in my mind the Lord would help me, I thought in my heart I would hate it. Nobody likes being sent to the principal's office, and I would have to be the principal. Bill, the headmaster, explained my responsibilities would be much more than simply those of a principal. As Director of Instruction, I would be in charge of what he called "quality control" (all the teaching that went on in the school: from teaching of academics to teaching of behavior management, from assessment to curriculum, from instructional strategies and approaches to study skill tips).

Having never started a school before, I relied a great deal on Bill, who had experience in that area. He was a wonderful mentor for me. But neither of us had ever started a school that began so big and grew so fast. During the spring before our first year, Bill was interviewing most of the prospective students and their parents. He was also hiring our staff. I was given the responsibility of ordering everything we would need (from textbooks, to AV equipment, to teaching aids, to office supplies, to consumable student materials, and more). It was my job to set up our special education program (by writing the budget for it, hiring the teacher and the aide, screening all the applicants, developing all our forms, selecting the curriculum, etc.). We both had "a million details" to attend to.

I'll never forget one day in May before the fall of our first year. As I was literally walking out the door Bill asked to look at my 'To Do' list. As he compared his to mine, he concluded I was in better shape than he was to handle a few "little" projects. In one breath he asked me to write the report cards, write all the fire escape routes for each classroom, and develop the scope and sequence (the framework) for our Bible curriculum. I sat down and didn't know whether to laugh, cry, or vomit. Seated behind a partition, I couldn't see who was standing just outside the office. My response to developing the scope and sequence for our Bible curriculum was to blurt out, "I'd have to read the whole Bible!" Having overheard that, one of our pastors walked in and said, "Well it wouldn't hurt!"

By then I had changed jobs five years in a row. My career was taking off. It was as if the Lord was preparing me to help begin a Christian school as an administrator. With the school beginning large and growing strong (to about 700 students by our third year!), I was extremely busy and very happy. I was content and thankful that all was going well for Chris and our family.

My thoughts during Chris's early high school years were, "Why me?" Knowing God promises that in this world we will have tribulation, I wondered why God was being so merciful during those years of newfound joy. Happy times during this period of our lives included elaborate Easter scavenger hunts designed to challenge and entertain two very bright teenagers. The Chandler family had gone high tech. and purchased several computers (which were frequently used simultaneously for schoolwork by Robert, Chris, and me). When the boys were younger, Howie played board games with them. With so many challenging software programs available, the guys spent lots of "male bonding" time playing games on the computer.

We started going to the movies. As avid movie buffs, we had it down to an art: we'd buy the tickets hours ahead of time, we'd sit on the left side of the theater, we developed a friendly game to occupy ourselves while we waited for the movie to start (seeing who could give the most correct names of the movies previewed), etc.

My extended family provided happy times, as well. They would plan elaborate theme parties and invite lots of family and friends. The road rallies we had involved fireworks, good food, and prizes for just about every category imaginable (which led to some serious competition!). For example, the first year we had a road rally, my car won the prize for being the messiest (for which I lodged an official complaint, because I had come straight from camp!). In addition, my sister-in-law and I won a prize for being the best dressed. So, the following year we came with a car that was spotless inside and out. We even bought spray that made the interior smell like it was brand new. I wore a chauffeur's outfit. As we drove up to my cousin's house, I let my family members out of the car. The following year someone outdid me by coming dressed as the Statue of Liberty. As her car drove up my cousin's long driveway, we could see her standing perfectly still, extending out of her sunroof with her arm holding the torch stretched out majestically in the air!

I also noticed prizes were awarded to children who attended the road rally that were injured (some had casts). One year I decided to show up "injured" figuring I'd win at least one prize. Just before we drove up the driveway, I wrapped gauze around my head, over my eyes (but I could really see through it). I had my arm in a sling, too. As we approached the other ralliers, I drove up the driveway swerving, with my family members screaming directions out the window to me.

Prior to our first trip to Disney World, we had a get-together that involved a Disney World trivia competition between two teams. My cousin made up the "test," complete with questions specifically only for the younger team members.

Life just seemed too good to be true.

Chapter 6
Typical Adolescence or A Mother's Intuition?

When Chris was in eleventh grade, he became an assistant squad leader in the marching band. During the summer, when I dropped him off at band camp, he just didn't look right. He would stare at me with a helpless, almost fearful look as I'd drive away. Then when I'd pick him up, he didn't seem right. It was as if he was relieved for some reason. I knew social skills were a challenge to him and, because of his leadership position, he was forced to interact with his peers. He had to command the respect of his squad members and get them to cooperate. Although the band had a great bunch of kids, they were all still teenagers. It was difficult to ascertain if he was changing due to adolescence or if something was really wrong. There was no use asking Chris; he didn't want me to pry. Asking him questions might have implied that I thought he needed my advice on how he should be a leader. So I was left to wonder. Rather, I was left to try not to wonder.

I had enough things on my mind anyway. At my work "busy" took on a whole new meaning for me. I was totally absorbed in my job. I convinced myself I was a good role model for the boys by being dedicated to my ministry (working 14 hours a day — 10 at school and 4 on paper work at home). In the fall of 1996 I found out I was on the borderline for developing Diabetes. My mother had a brother who died of Diabetes, so there was a hereditary predisposition. In addition, years of high carbohydrate diet had resulted in my being overweight. The doctor said I needed to do three things to prevent Diabetes: lose weight, exercise, and change my lifestyle by reducing stress (busy and worry stress). Chris was just learning to drive, and three months later he had a breakdown. No stress there!!

In the fall of that year Robert, Chris's best friend, spent every night on the phone with a "girlfriend" and Howie spent most of his time at home helping out with the chores. Chris was in his junior year and had several honors courses and one Advanced Placement (college level) course. He knew that the colleges mostly look at the grades during the junior year in high school. So, he spent most of his time at home in his bedroom (I assumed doing homework). He was pushing himself to maintain all A's and B's. He didn't smile as much as he used to, but I chalked that up to a teenage attitude.

Chris knew I needed to lose weight for health reasons. Since I was put on the "Fen-Phen" diet, I was quickly losing weight. Later, I discovered Chris thought I was dying. No one could have predicted what was to come (out of a life that seemed to be just coming together). There were no obvious warning signals. I suppose I should have been more aware of Chris being at high risk of becoming mentally ill. Many people ask me what caused his breakdown. As I look back, I can easily see there was a combination of contributing factors:

- Family history of mental illness
- ADHD (at higher risk of developing mental illness)
- Significant past hurts
- Mounting pressures
- Hormonal changes (he went through a tremendous growth spurt)

However, at that time I was thankful everything seemed fine. Perhaps, I should have listened more to my intuition, but I didn't spend emotional energy on unnecessary feelings of guilt. I gave myself the advice I had given other parents: don't look back, except to remember what God had done. Also, I told myself, as I told others, that since I had done the best I could and never intended to harm my son, there was no need to feel guilt.

Chapter 7
The Unthinkable and The Unbearable

It was about two weeks before Christmas. After a busy day at school I was trying to relax a few minutes before the next part of my day: making dinner, spending time with the family, and getting ready for Christmas (cards, shopping, wrapping, etc.). After dinner Chris came into the kitchen and sat down as if to talk with me. With everything I had to do I really didn't have time for a chat with my son. So I proceeded to share some small talk as I finished up the dishes. Chris's responses seemed distant. He seemed serious and preoccupied with something he needed to discuss. So I realized I needed to re-evaluate my priorities for the evening. I sat down and asked him what he wanted to talk about. With tears in his eyes he said, "Mom, I'm lonely."

Immediately I felt a pain pierce my heart like a knife severing all my emotions. I knew all the abuse he had endured through the years — the emotional pain from thoughtless teachers who demeaned his dignity, and the physical and emotional pain inflicted by his peers. However, I had convinced myself none of it really bothered him because he never showed any sadness or expressed any loneliness. I reasoned that he must have gotten desensitized to the way he was treated by others, or he never really was fully paying attention to the tormenting in the first place. I hoped he had forgotten most of the ugly experiences, and that time had healed his hurts. And I rationalized that since he's a male, he probably didn't hurt as much as a mother hurts for her child. And yet I had just learned there was something worse than being tormented by your peers. It's worse to be ignored by your peers, especially when you're a teenager and you want so desperately to be included. During marching band season I watched the entire band (which included the nicest bunch of kids in the high school) walk past Chris as though he didn't exist. I watched as Chris would try to speak to a fellow band member and be ignored as though he were invisible. The worst part was watching Robert surrounded by a crowd of friends — he was popular and he wasn't including his brother, either. And yet, I couldn't fault Robert for having a happy adolescence. Lord only knows how Robert stuck by his brother so many years.

As I heard those words "I'm lonely" echo in my mind, I realized all the pain from the past never went away. I knew he would have to deal with quite a bit of rejection and emotional scars. But I had no idea how I was going to go through it with him. I could barely deal with watching my son hurt the first times around; how could I relive all those terrible memories?

I sat there and talked with Chris for about two hours. After that I went upstairs and told Howie what was happening. We thought everything was fine with Chris, but deep down inside him he was torn apart. I told Howie he would have to help me help Chris because I was beyond sucking fumes emotionally — that I didn't have anything left — I just couldn't deal with it alone any more.

The next night Chris needed to talk again. This time Howie and I together listened to him, comforted him, affirmed him, and prayed with him. That was a Thursday night.

The following night, Friday, the boys had a performance at school. They were both in several bands and had a busy night ahead of them. I had to get dinner ready quickly. We had to eat. They had to locate all the parts of their tuxedos and get dressed for the concert. Chris came over to me while I was making dinner. Knowing I had devoted two whole nights to him just recently, I felt it was Okay for me to tell him I couldn't talk with him at that moment. He wouldn't stop talking to me. I was feeling overwhelmed with the details of life. At the same time, I was a little upset that Chris would be so demanding of my time. And, yet, I knew in my heart Chris was hurting and sensed he was reaching out. But I told him to let me make dinner. He walked away, annoyed.

After the concert Chris made an odd and insulting comment to a fellow female musician. He also told her mother the comment (that she should play louder). That was so unlike Chris. He normally

62464422426

was very complimentary and nonassertive. In the car, he told me what he had said to them. I began to be a little alarmed, but couldn't figure out why he said those things. It wasn't until the next night that I knew things were very wrong. Chris wouldn't stop talking to me and his comments were becoming more and more negative and unreasonable. Even though I told him to be quiet, he wouldn't stop talking. When Howie heard Chris talking after I told him to be quiet, he told Chris to obey me and stop talking. Chris kept on talking. We both wound up yelling at him to be quiet.

Later on Saturday night Chris spoke very strangely to a girl he knew quite well. He and Robert went to the movies with two girls. Coming home in the car, the girl who was with Chris was in tears and Howie heard parts of what he was saying. It was judgmental and cruel.

At church on Sunday morning Chris was acting very strange. He insisted on talking to the guest speaker after the service. I was positive something was wrong. Weeks later I learned the senior youth pastor has seen Chris that morning and knew what was wrong — Chris was about to have a total mental breakdown. So Sunday night all the pastors were praying for Chris even before I had asked for prayer. That was just a perfect example of how God knows what we want even before we ask.

By Sunday night Chris was talking non-stop. There was no conversation. He didn't acknowledge our comments in any way. His thoughts were so distorted and disconnected. Having been in the field of special education, I knew what was happening. I knew what had to be done and what our future might hold. I knew Chris would need medication and would probably need to be hospitalized. I also knew if he was schizophrenic we might never see him restored back to reality. I knew he could be very violent and unpredictable. I knew I had to get help for him. I had to explain it all to Howie, but it was hard for Howie to understand what I was saying. If you've never had any exposure to this sort of thing, it's hard to understand. As a parent it's hard to accept. God created us with emotions that cushion us.

We often fall into denial as a form of emotional shock so we can function when things are most critical. Later, when we can deal with the horrifying emotions, the denial goes away and other feelings emerge.

As I watched Chris ramble on distorting the words in the Bible and pacing the floor as a caged animal, I couldn't help but think I was witnessing the result of all those years of pain. I saw before me a broken young man, a son in torment, a "gifted" mind that was gone. I knew only a few days before I had fully believed I couldn't face any more pain and now I was going to have to face something far worse than ever. I resolved in my mind and in my heart that the Lord was going to have to help me. I was going to need supernatural peace and strength and wisdom and patience. I knew I was trained to deal with significant emotional and behavior problems, and so once again I would bear the burden rather than Howie. I can't explain how it happened that I instantly received the peace I needed, but I did. I suppose God honored the fact that I knew He was able to provide all I needed, and I never once questioned Him. It would have been easy to engage in a pity party, curse God, and shrink from reality myself. But just as Paul in the Bible said, I had learned to be content in whatever circumstance I was in. I had seen how God used my past trials to help me minister to other parents and how He used those trials to help me be a better teacher and administrator. So I wasn't about to question God now. I knew I simply had to lean on Him. Suddenly, the second part of a familiar verse had new meaning for me: "The peace that passeth understanding shall guard your heart and mind..."

Chapter 8
"Are You Still Alive?"

The next day was a work day. My plan was to take Chris to school where there was a psychologist on our church staff. Although I knew Chris needed to be hospitalized, I wanted him to be under Christian care. Somehow I got Chris dressed and out in the car and took him with me to my school. As I drove I explained to Chris what was happening. I doubted he was even coherent enough to understand what I was saying, but I felt I owed it to him to treat him with dignity, even in his condition. I explained that he's probably mentally ill and that he'll need some medicine to help him feel better mentally. I told him I would take him to talk to a psychologist and he would need to be seen by a physician and by a psychiatrist. As I drove to school that morning, I reminded myself my own father had experienced a breakdown when I was growing up. I assured myself everything would be Okay just like they were with my father who lived a full, successful, and happy life (on medication for depression).

It was a Monday morning. Since our classrooms were used by the church on Sundays, our headmaster, Bill, went around the building every Monday morning checking what needed to be done and who needed help getting their rooms in order for the students. Chris wandered into the building slowly behind me. As I approached the office area, Bill approached me. I asked him, "Do you have a minute?" He briskly answered, "That's just about all I have!" I proceeded into his office passing him. He turned and followed me into his office, sensing I had something serious to tell him. I simply said, "Chris's mind has snapped. He's lost it." Bill asked where he was. I told him I brought him in so the psychologist, Jack, could see him. Bill told me to take Chris home and they would call me when Jack came in.

When we got home I went directly to take our dog out. When I glanced at her I saw her eyes were both totally bloodshot and swollen, almost bleeding. She was also wet. As I looked at her,

Chris said he put her in the shower to get the blood off. He said he slapped her because she wouldn't sit still when he asked her to; she kept going for the dog yummy. Then I realized Chris had kept her in the bathroom with him during the night. During the night I laid awake listening, not sure what Chris was doing. All I heard was him in the bathroom a lot. I remember him taking about five showers. I had gotten up several times to check on him and he was in the bathroom. I didn't hear anything and assumed he fell asleep, so I went back to bed, never realizing that Zelda (our dog) wasn't in our bedroom.

An hour after I got home I received a call from Jack telling me he was at church and I could bring Chris over. When I got to the church, the secretaries told me Jack wanted to talk to me first and to let Chris wait in their office. I was concerned because I knew he had harmed Zelda and wasn't sure what he'd do, although he didn't seem threatening to other people or me. After Jack and I talked briefly, Jack brought Chris in. Jack began to ask Chris a few questions. It was apparent Chris couldn't follow the conversation. I could tell that Chris was trying as hard as he could to answer Jack, because there was some exchange, but then Chris would go off onto some other distorted thought. When Jack asked Chris if he was hearing any voices, Chris said, "Yes." I knew that was an indication of schizophrenia. I didn't know if I could go on hearing any more. Jack asked what the voices were saying. Chris told him the voices were Jack's! Thank God!! I was so relieved that I enjoyed the humor in it.

After a short time Jack concluded that Chris, indeed, was having a psychotic episode (sometimes referred to as a 'nervous breakdown'). He said we should take Chris to a physician to decide what the next step would be.

We drove to Dr. Kent's office. The nurses had Chris and me wait in one of the treatment rooms. An unsuspecting nurse came in to check Chris's blood pressure. Casually, she asked, "So...why are we here today?" Much to my surprise and to hers, Chris responded,

"Because I'm mentally ill." The nurse looked at me with an inquisitive look as if to say, "Is that right?" and I nodded, yes. She quickly got his blood pressure (which was soaring) and left the room. The next thing that happened was that Dr. Kent and Jack came into the room. After a brief observation, Dr. Kent said he was going to prescribe medication to stabilize him. He explained the first thing we needed to do was to get Chris stabilized — to bring him back to reality. Then we'd begin dealing with what caused the episode. As he spoke to me I could tell on their faces that this was serious. Although I knew fully what was happening, it all seemed surreal. The expressions on their faces helped me realize this was really happening. As I expected, they said he should be hospitalized, but we should try to avoid that if at all possible. They asked me if I was willing to try to stabilize him at home. I agreed. I knew it would be up to me and me alone. Since Chris was so unstable, it was risky to have him around people — even his own family. I knew it would be best to have Howie go to work and to have Robert go to school. I also knew that, even though I would do my best to create a safe environment at home, I couldn't protect myself from a young man who was bigger, stronger, and smarter than I was and who had a black belt in karate. The Lord, Himself, would have to keep all of us safe.

I have a very dear friend, Jane, who is my mentor and who is a certified school nurse. I managed to call her because she would want to know what was going on. She was very concerned for my safety and for the family's safety. I assured her Chris was receiving intensive out patient care and we were in touch with the physician and psychologist every day. She and I both knew, however, I should have been in contact with a psychiatrist and Chris should be in the hospital. She heard his voice and could tell it didn't sound at all like Chris. Even his eyes had a sort of emptiness. She and I both knew people as unstable as he was are capable of extreme violence. She promised she would call me every day to make sure I was still alive.

What is a day in the life of a mother like whose son is out of touch with reality? For ten days I didn't sleep at nights, I only rested.

I took very brief showers at night when my husband was home. I hid all our knives, scissors, matches, medicine, and anything else I thought could be a weapon or harmful to Chris or us. I had to keep track of where our dog was at all times without Chris realizing it. I had to maintain a calm demeanor no matter what Chris's emotions were at the time. He would go from hugging me to sobbing, saying "Why me? I didn't do anything wrong" to shouting and breaking walls and mirrors or slamming doors.

I recall one incident when Chris karate-kicked a mirror and broke it. As I sat on the floor cleaning up the broken glass I was sobbing. It was like picking up the broken pieces of his life. It was so hard to watch my son, broken, doing things so unlike him. It was as if all his pain from so many years was being unleashed. I knew it was difficult for Robert, too. Life was anything but normal, and he had to go to school acting as if everything was fine. There was no way for me to shield him from what he had to see at night. As Robert was getting ready for bed that night, he literally had to step around the broken glass and his weeping mother.

We witnessed Chris destroying other things because he said they were "evil." He had taken Robert's Casio keyboard and totally destroyed the controls. I had to endure the constant playing of "Jesus Christ Superstar" (the opera). Chris played it over and over and over again until I thought I would lose my mind. I couldn't take the CD away until I felt he wouldn't become violent looking for it. After I hid the CD, I heard Chris playing the opera on the piano. Even Robert begged me to do something to make him stop playing that music. Chris also played "Joy to the World" in a dissonant tone. He kept saying when he played it regularly, the world would end. One day he got his trumpet and yelled at me to turn on the TV. With urgency in his voice he said, "Here it comes!!! Get ready! The world will end now!" At that moment I didn't know what he meant by that or what he intended to do. Thankfully, nothing happened. Oddly enough, his musical abilities never left him. He played the piano and the trumpet all day, but all in a distorted dissonant tone. It was as if he had found a creative outlet for his misery. And I heard it all day long.

I had to listen to Chris talk to me with the most bazaar comments. He kept asking me what the Bible said about certain things. Because his mind was racing, he demanded to know exactly what the Bible said immediately after he asked me. I couldn't find the verses fast enough. Even though I was extremely frustrated, I couldn't yell at him or give up. Either of those two responses would have gotten him angry and perhaps violent. He twisted the words in the Bible, saying he was the archangel. At one point he ripped the back of a white shirt and tied it around his neck to represent his wings. He carried his Bible everywhere and preached nonstop. We had to stop speaking about the Lord because that would just feed his distorted thinking. I never realized how much a part of my every day conversations the Lord was. So I hid all of our Bibles (never realizing we had so many!) I even had to hide all our phones because the mother of the girl from the movies said Chris called their house at 2:00 AM to apologize. I had to deal with my own son standing inches away from me holding a screwdriver saying, "I could kill you with this. You know I could kill you for having me." I also had to deal with the fact that Robert thought his brother (as he knew him) was gone, and I couldn't guarantee Chris would come back to reality or ever be like he used to be.

Chris's blood pressure remained high as long as his mind kept racing. Often his nose would start bleeding. When I was a child the artery in my nose grew before my nose did and so it would break and I would get nosebleeds that wouldn't stop until I got my nose cauterized. Since I got so many bloody noses as a child, I knew what did and didn't work to make the bleeding stop. When Chris got his first bloody nose, I began to tell him what to do. This was perceived as controlling to him and he resisted. He even did the opposite of what I told him to do. If I told him to breathe out of his mouth, he blew forcefully out of his nose causing blood to spray out. It was so frustrating and upsetting, I began to cry; he wouldn't do anything to make it stop. We were in the bathroom. At one point Chris shook his head and the blood flew all around the bathroom splattering on the walls. It looked like a murder scene. I knew if I didn't leave the bathroom it would never stop bleeding. I had to walk away, and hope and pray that he would stop it on his own.

Each day I had to keep anecdotal records and document what was going on to help the professionals identify what was going on with Chris. I had to administer his medication (Risperdal). It was important for me to follow the doctor's specific instructions to alter the dosage of the medication each day. We quickly spiked the dosage in the first few days, and then lowered the dosage as he became more stabilized. Every time I gave him his medication, he would get agitated. No one can comprehend what it means to be out of touch with reality. So Chris could not believe that he suddenly had a breakdown. All he knew was one day his life was fine and the next he was having trouble thinking and his mother was giving him some medication. The obvious conclusion for him was that I was causing him to have trouble thinking. One day Howie gave Chris some over-the-counter medication the doctor said to get to help calm Chris down. The problem was I had just administered an increased dosage of the Risperdal. I was out in the car taking Chris to see some Christmas lights and Chris began to get extremely agitated. He started pounding the dashboard. Then he put his head back saying his tongue was swollen. He was shouting and crying. It was all I could do to safely get us home. I had to call the psychologist and physician every day. I couldn't allow the radio or TV to be on because most of what was on would feed his distorted thoughts or make him angry. I struggled to find something that I could do. I found that household chores lent themselves to calm and productive activities.

What does a mother think and feel when her son is out of touch with reality? I wondered what precipitated the breakdown. Yet I knew he had a hereditary predisposition to it, he had experienced great emotional hurts in the past, that individuals with ADHD are at greater risk of becoming mentally ill, and that he was under a lot of pressure. I worried I would have to hear about something horrific that had happened to Chris. I also imagined what it would be like if Chris stabbed me. I remember hearing on the news when people have been stabbed, it sometimes feels like you've been punched and you don't initially realize you've been stabbed. So I convinced myself it wouldn't be so bad if he stabbed me. I thought about how I would feel if he killed himself. I knew the loss would be devastating, but the Lord would sustain us as He had through other trials. I even thought I'd be happy for Chris to finally be out of the world that had been so miserable to him for most of his life. I marveled at how the Lord was enabling me to go on for days without sleep, under extreme sorrow and yet remaining calm, flooding my head with Bible verses of assurance.

Incidentally, a few days after Chris had his breakdown, Robert broke his ankle in wrestling. That surely complicated our lives! Howie had to take him to get the X-rays. Once again I couldn't be with Robert when he had a broken bone and needed me. It was one more thing that potentially upset Chris, who was already thinking the world is unfair. When Robert first injured his ankle, the trainer told him it probably wasn't broken and he could walk on it. The trainer only gave him one crutch, so it was hard for Robert to stay off it. When I told Robert we would have to take him to get X-rays, Robert argued with me, telling me the trainer had already told him it probably wasn't broken. My emotions were raging inside. With Chris listening to the whole conversation, I was mindful that Robert's injury and our arguing could set him off. But there I stood with both my sons hurting and rejecting my care. I stood my ground and insisted Robert get X-rays. It was a learning experience for Robert to find out that mothers can be right! It angered me that a trainer would hint at a diagnosis and then only give Robert one crutch, as though his own diagnosis was correct.

As I looked for God's purpose in allowing Robert to break his ankle, I realized it was something concrete for Chris to see that could be used as an example to him. I used it to explain that just like

Robert's ankle had broken, it was as if Chris's mind had suffered an injury. And just like Robert needed a cast to support his leg while it healed, Chris needed medication and people to support him while his mind healed. I also related Chris's illness to an electric fuse box. I told him people could blow a fuse by having too much electrical stress on one electrical line. The system is designed to shut down before something worse happens. I related that to how his mind shut down so nothing worse would happen. Then I continued with the analogy by explaining we simply need to rewire his system. I told him we would create a new and stronger cable that could handle a great deal of stress in the future. The cable would be made up of many "wires" (prayer, talking to others and not 'stuffing' emotions any more, and medication).

In the midst of Chris's breakdown and Robert's broken ankle, we could still keep a sense of humor. Robert and I were talking about the recent health problems in our family: my impaired glucose tolerance, Chris's breakdown, and Robert's broken ankle. I commented sarcastically, "Doesn't anyone in this family know how to get attention the right way?!" We also teased about how the house rules in situations such as this included the rule that only one person could have a breakdown at a time.

Several days later Robert needed X-rays again because the doctor thought he might have pneumonia. It turned out all he had was bronchitis. But nonetheless, he did have a broken bone. So I had to pick him up from school each day. Fortunately, for most of the six weeks he had his cast on, Chris was stabilized and I could leave him alone briefly. However, Chris was upset each time I went to get Robert because I took Zelda. He was angry that even our dog could get out and take a ride to school and he couldn't.

Robert and Chris were scheduled to go to San Antonio, Texas, to perform with their marching band at the Alamo Bowl over the Christmas vacation. Obviously, Chris would be unable to go. During the ten days Chris was experiencing his psychotic episode, there was a dress rehearsal for the trip. We had to get Robert out of the house without Chris seeing him. I knew if Chris saw Robert leave in his uniform, he would expect to go to the rehearsal, too. And if I had to tell him he couldn't, I was afraid he would get agitated or even violent. Thankfully, we were successful and there wasn't an incident. However, several nights later, little did I know that just before Howie took Robert out somewhere, he told Chris he wouldn't be going on his trip to Texas. Moments after Howie and Robert left the house, Chris came downstairs with his shirt tied tightly around his neck as a tourniquet with his face beat red and his eyes bulging. He walked over near our trophy case that was all glass. I was alone with him — he was suicidal and unpredictable. That was one of the times I was most vulnerable and in danger. The Lord protected me and helped me to remain calm and to speak calmly to Chris. I didn't have the luxury of getting angry with Howie; I was dealing with too many emotions at the time (Chris's and mine). Even then the Lord helped me to realize Howie simply didn't understand the serious nature of Chris's illness. Several weeks later there was another incident that made it clear to me Howie didn't understand the danger I was in. But my friend Jane did and she continued to call me every day just to ask, "Are you still alive?"

Chapter 9
Two Months in the Fire

With inexpressible joy and relief, we watched as Chris became stabilized just in time for Christmas Eve. Finally, I could leave Chris in the hands of Howie and go to church. It was an amazing thing to realize the Lord had helped me to keep going for ten days without one full night of sleep keeping my mind alert and my emotions calm. Finally, I knew we would once again be able to have a normal conversation with our son. No matter what his illness was, nothing else mattered. An experience like that sure has a way of helping you re-evaluate your priorities. We told Chris we didn't care if he went to college or not. The only requirements we had were that he didn't hurt himself or anyone else. Actually, the experience forced us to shift our focus from the temporal things of this world to eternal things. All that was important was that Chris was getting better and we were all alive.

Prior to Chris's illness, Howie and I had planned a trip to Williamsburg, Virginia. We were going to go away while the boys were in Texas. Now that we knew Chris was stabilized, we didn't have to cancel our trip. We made arrangements to take Chris with us. Our purpose of the trip no longer was for Howie and me to get away for a romantic week; we were taking our son on a trip to minister to him.

The trip in the car to Virginia was long. Under the direction of the physician, Chris still had to take his Risperdal. Now that Chris was stabilized, I could tell the medication was interfering with his ADHD. It was making him more hyperactive and he couldn't sleep much. It was extremely difficult for Chris to sit still. I can only liken it to when adults have to endure several hours in a college course or a long sermon. Eventually, you almost want to jump out of your skin or run out of the room. I could tell that being in the car was a kind of torture for Chris. As we drove on the 65-mile-an-hour highway, we passed blue signs for rest stops. As we passed each blue sign, Chris begged us to stop at the rest stop. Knowing it was difficult for him to sit still for a long time, we agreed to stop every time he requested it. In my opinion, Virginia has way too many rest stops!!! Chris spotted every sign. I thought we would never reach Williamsburg. I began to pray he wouldn't notice every blue sign. Thankfully, Chris missed seeing one and we drove for a longer stretch without stopping. But it became unbearable for Chris. All of a sudden Chris said, "I'm gonna step out for a minute." As though choreographed, Howie and I instantly and simultaneously pushed the button that locks all the doors in the car. Then we both said casually (hiding our panic) and in unison, "What did you say?" Now that we can look back on it, we can laugh at it. But that was one indication of how unpredictable Chris was even after he was stabilized.

Being in Williamsburg was kind of like a celebration that our son was restored. It brought to mind the story of the prodigal son in the Bible, and we could imagine what joy the father of the prodigal son experienced. It had to be sheer elation! I couldn't stop looking at Chris because his normal expression had returned to him. I kept taking pictures of him all week. Several months later we took Chris to Longwood Gardens and once again I took lots of pictures of him. While posing for a picture, Chris said with a note of sarcasm, "And here's Chris after his breakdown..." That was his way of kindly saying he was tired of it all and that was enough pictures.

Sometimes the Master Potter allows us (His pottery) to go through the fire. I am told the hotter the furnace is, the more radiant the vessel is when the pottery is removed from the furnace. It was God's plan for me to spend two months with Chris "in the fire" where we experienced sorrow and God's love at the same time.

When we returned from Williamsburg I knew the crisis wasn't over. There was much that needed to be done. We had to determine what was wrong with Chris, determine how to effectively treat him, begin to address his emotional pain, and prepare him for going back to school (if that was possible). I arranged for "out patient" therapy for Chris. That involved regular, weekly visits to see a psychiatrist and psychologist. The Lord helped me locate the Christian psychologist, Dr. Kipley, who Chris had seen when he was in fifth grade. That was a real blessing because Dr. Kipley knew Chris and his history. It was Dr. Kipley that recommended Dr. Newman, a Christian psychiatrist and neurologist. It was amazing that God provided two Christian professionals who were so capable and nearby.

When I first took Chris to see the psychiatrist, Dr. Newman began asking Chris some questions. He asked Chris if he was hearing voices. Once again (like in Jack's office) Chris answered, "Yes." I watched as Dr. Newman seriously jotted a few notes in response. I knew he was thinking that Chris was schizophrenic, and I secretly enjoyed the momentary humor. I knew what the next question would be. Dr. Newman then asked Chris what the voices were saying. Chris said, "You should know. I'm hearing your voice."

While in Williamsburg I hadn't slept much because Chris (who was in our room) was restless. I was still functioning on strength from the Lord mixed with exuberance. Once home, however, it was time for me to get some sleep. It occurred to me to give Chris some Excedrin PM and to take some myself. I knew I needed sleep badly and so I took two pills.

Before I went to sleep I instructed Howie to wake me up in the morning before he went to work if Chris was awake. The next morning I awoke to find Chris up. I called Howie to find out how long Chris had been awake. I asked him if Chris was awake when Howie was still home. Howie told me Chris was awake early in the morning before he left for work. I asked Howie why he didn't wake me up. Howie explained he had tried to wake me up, but he couldn't. I explained it wasn't safe for me to be alone in the house when Chris was awake and I was asleep.

That night I took some Excedrin again. The same thing happened. I awoke to find Chris awake and found out Howie had tried to wake me up, but couldn't. Then I realized Howie still didn't comprehend the danger. I suppose most parents can't imagine that their own son could harm them or even kill them. But my training and experience helped me to realize the very real danger. So I proceeded to spell out what could happen. I told Howie if he wouldn't do whatever it took to wake me up, he'd better prepare himself to come home to find a dead wife and a missing son. I also rehearsed with him the procedure we'd have to follow if Chris managed to stab me and I'd be able to call Howie. I told Howie it would be important to call our pastors so they could get to our house before the police to ensure Chris would be taken to a hospital instead of to jail. That was the last time Howie left the house without making sure I was awake. But that wasn't the last time Chris threatened to kill me by stabbing me (or himself)!

Even though Chris was threatening to harm himself and me, the psychologist and psychiatrist didn't feel he would really carry it out. They both, however, urged us to get him into the hospital and on medication. But that was easier said than done. Chris would threaten to kill me if I took him to the hospital or put him on medication again (at that point he had been taken off the Risperdal).

My days were filled with observing odd and bizarre behaviors and hearing distorted thoughts. Whenever Chris held Zelda, he hugged her tightly until she squirmed to get away. Then he would growl at her. Zelda's tolerance for him was unbelievable. It was as if she, too, knew Chris was really sick. Chris read only Revelation in the Bible and then insisted I listen to his (twisted) interpretation of it. Chris thought I was the Virgin Mary and he was the archangel. He also thought he literally had lost his mind. That almost made sense to me, since people often say, "I'm going to lose my mind." I can't imagine exactly what it's like to have a breakdown, but I'm sure it must feel like you really have lost your mind. One day when I took him to the doctor Chris saw a man in the parking lot and thought he was Einstein. Chris also began cursing, saying words that were never uttered in our house. It was strange and shocking (even to Robert) to hear what flew out of his mouth with ease. At dinner he wouldn't eat meat. When I encouraged him to eat meat, he would take a bite and swallow it whole glaring at me with an empty look in his eyes. I had to look beyond the cold stare in his eyes, reminding myself he was my son who was simply sick. The more bizarre Chris was, the angrier I became at the enemy. I knew Jesus had already won the victory over sin and death on the cross. I knew Jesus would help us through any trial. With spiritual assurance I claimed the verse that we are "more than conquerors." When Chris was his weakest, I knew the Lord was strong (and He could make me strong). In the face of a situation that could have easily caused tremendous anguish and despair, I experienced an amazing assurance and determination. I was surely experiencing an astonishing mystery. I can't imagine how anyone could endure what I was able to withstand without God's help.

One of Chris's unusual behaviors was that he threw away money. One day he came into my bedroom and put a pile of bills and coins on my floor and told me I could have it all. Then he took one bill back and left the room. Somehow I knew he planned to burn it. I followed him downstairs and saw him setting the bill on fire at the stove. Had I not been right there at that instant, we could have had a fire.

Since Chris's behavior was so unpredictable, I had to watch him at all times, or at least know what he was doing. That wasn't easy to do because I had to stay near him without him thinking I was following him. If he knew I was following him, he might think I didn't trust him, and then get agitated. So I had to get creative in my reasons for walking around the house (doing chores, looking for something, coming to ask him a question, looking for Zelda to take her out, etc.).

It was hard for me to know how Chris was feeling. This wasn't like a physical illness that could be measured. Even the psychiatrist said it was very difficult to know exactly what was causing Chris's behavior at different times. His behavior could have been attributed to: mood swings (hypomania), psychosis, typical teenage behavior, his breakdown (paranoia can result), his ADHD, his intelligence (saying or doing what he thought we wanted), his unique personality, etc. So, I devised a way to get some more objective information from him. I invented a stress meter, a barometer of levels of stress. I explained that on a scale of 1-10, 10 was the most stress anyone can experience. Then I asked him how much stress he was under just before his breakdown. He told me, "About seven or eight." Then I asked him what would be a normal stress level — the average amount of stress that people typically experience — and he told me "About three." So whenever I wanted to know how he was feeling, I'd simply ask him, "What's your level?" and he knew what I meant.

Another problem I had to solve was how to help Chris understand that I loved him no matter what he did or didn't do. So one night I explained to him that I was proud of him because of who he was, not because of anything he had done. I listed all the things I loved about him, that made him special. I knew it was important for him to hear all the different ways God had made him special (his mathematical mind, his love for pondering things, his charming personality that enables him to relate well to adults, his love for the Lord, his determination and ability to be goal-oriented, his talent for paying attention to several things at once, his musical gift, his dry sense of humor, his thankful and appreciative spirit, his willingness to take risks, etc.). It was important not to mention accomplishments, because then he would feel he had to earn my love. He needed to know there was a lot about him that I could affirm, even if he never gets recognition from anyone for it. Every night when I put him to bed I said, "I'm proud of you, Chris. Why?" He was supposed to answer, "Because of who I am." That was the way we ended each day (after prayer and the reading of a Psalm). Sometimes I added, "I'm happy I had you." That seemed to mean a lot to him. I think he felt like he had let me down in some way and he was a failure. Mental illness can rob a person of truth and joy.

In order to pass the time, I rented Nintendo games and movies for Chris. I couldn't leave him alone. So I took him with me to the movie rental store every day. It was quite a challenge to manage him out in public. I had to keep him calm, near me, and away from anything that might upset him. I also had to keep him away from any video tapes that would reinforce his psychotic thinking. It amazed me how many movies had come out at that time about angels!

After about six weeks at home with Chris, he still wasn't much better. I tried to look for any little signs of improvement, but then we would visit the psychologist or the psychiatrist and they would inform me he was still far from getting better. I became tired and quite discouraged. It was hard for me to remain positive. When a young mother is around a toddler who talks "baby talk" all day, she begins to think and talk that way too. Being around someone with distorted thoughts made it difficult for me to think clearly myself. Whenever Chris seemed fairly content and occupied, I'd go to the phone and call work. It was helpful for me to think about my responsibilities there. It was mentally stimulating for me. One day, however, Bill told me to stop calling work and focus on Chris. I obeyed him and began to fall into depression myself, after a week of focusing only on distorted thoughts. I convinced Bill that it helped me to call work, so he allowed it under specific conditions. He had my best interest in mind and wanted to do anything that would help. It was wonderful to just call and talk to my secretary who was an excellent listener. She was very compassionate, and without me at work she had the time to listen.

There were moments that were very special, however. Whenever Chris had a positive mood swing, he appeared to be much happier. It was then that we could go places. I took him bowling one day. Another day, I took him out to eat at a restaurant. We also went to the movies. One night I took Chris to the store with me. As we were leaving the house, Chris asked me how I knew the Lord loved him — other than what the Bible said. That was such a difficult question for me to answer. I wasn't able to convince him in his depressed condition that the Lord loved him. So I asked the Lord to show him. As we returned home I noticed a beautiful sky. There were puffy white clouds lit up by the moonlight. There was an orange tint to the moon with a yellow ring around it.

Instantly, I realized the Lord was revealing His love to Chris in a very concrete way. I told Chris when a young child wants to show his love to his parent, he draws a lovely picture and presents it to his parent as an expression of his love. Then I told Chris to look up in the sky and I pointed out that God had painted him a beautiful picture to show His love for Chris.

Another way God demonstrated His love for Chris was through Zelda. Often Chris felt needless guilt for harming her. Zelda was reluctant to approach Chris because his behavior was so unusual and sometimes harmful to her. I explained that one reason God gives us dogs is to demonstrate unconditional love, similar to God's love for us. I encouraged Chris to call Zelda and then watch as she would come to him (even though he had mistreated her). I trusted that God would honor that example I offered Chris and have Zelda go to him. As soon as Chris called her name, Zelda happily went to him without any hesitation. Chris had another example of God's love for him. Chris also witnessed the outpouring of God's love through cards and letters that arrived every day from faithful Christians with words of encouragement and timely Bible verses.

During those long weeks we were still able to keep our sense of humor. For example, we often joked about a comment someone made about Robert who was still in a cast and on crutches. Robert went to the movies (with a girl!). When he came home he shared a comment an adult made when he was trying to get to his seat in the theater. Robert said an adult said to her husband, "Watch out for the handicapped boy." I began to console Robert saying at least he knows he won't be "handicapped" for long. Robert said he didn't mind the "handicapped" part; he resented being called a "boy!" He certainly had become an authentic teenager!!

During our conversation at dinner one night we enjoyed some spontaneous humor. The conversation was very intense at first. Chris was desperately trying to act and think like he used to. He turned to Robert and asked, "What did I used to do?" Robert rubbed the palms of his hands together, smiled, and said, "Well, you used to clean my room..." I was so proud of Robert that he could maintain a sense of humor through it all.

The expression, "When it rains, it pours" seemed to be an understatement in our family. During those two months, my sister became seriously ill, Howie had a minor car accident, our oven and refrigerator broke, and I fell and thought I had broken a bone, and I got a flat tire. I felt like wearing a sign that said, "Danger! Under attack — Stay away!"

Our senior pastor was wise enough to encourage Howie and me to get marital counseling. A crisis can either draw a couple together or separate a husband and wife. At first I didn't pursue counseling because I couldn't deal with any more in my life. Once our pastor found out we hadn't made the arrangements to come in for counseling, he called us and insisted we pick an evening. Since Chris could be left alone for a brief time with Robert, Howie and I began to go once a week. We found it was not simply helpful, but necessary.

In my heart I knew Chris wouldn't get better without medication, but I didn't know how I would be able to convince him to take any. My worst fear was that Chris would have to be hospitalized in order to receive proper treatment. After eight weeks at home alone with him, it became clear hospitalization was inevitable.

Chapter 10
Facing My Worst Fears

During the two months at home with Chris, he had periodic mood swings. His negative mood swings usually had a sad or depressed tone. But one week his negative mood swing was distinctly different. He seemed very angry and full of rage. It seemed like he wanted revenge. Things quickly escalated. I had taken him to the mall and was returning home in the car with him. When I pulled into the driveway, Chris stepped out and began to run away. I immediately ran into the house to get Howie to help find him. We both took off in different directions searching for him in the neighborhood. This was my worst nightmare. If Chris were in the hospital, I knew that would be awful for him, but he would be safe. If he killed himself, I knew he would be with the Lord. But if he remained lost, I wouldn't want to even imagine what he'd be going through (as an easy target for any one who preys on those most vulnerable). As I drove, I prayed. I stopped home to see if he had returned. I discovered he had returned, but left again. While he was home, he disrupted everything: he knocked Robert's drum set over, he dropped Robert's trombone on the floor (denting the bell), and he took one of our computers off the desk and placed it on the floor. I resumed my search in the car for Chris, wondering if our ordeal would ever end, and how it would end. I felt emptiness in the pit of my stomach. I stopped home again to find out a neighbor called to say Chris went to their house and was accusing us of abusing him. Thankfully, that neighbor called us and not the police. I suppose it was evident that Chris wasn't in his right mind.

That night Chris had an appointment with his psychologist. When he was in talking with Dr. Kipley, he began yelling at him and threatening him. Dr. Kipley advised us to get Chris into the hospital as soon as possible because he really was dangerous. But with Chris as dangerous as he was, I still didn't know how to get him to the hospital without him first harming me.

A few nights later we all went to the movies. When we returned home, Robert and Howie went upstairs. Chris approached me in the kitchen. He had an audiocassette tape in his hand. He broke it in front of me saying that was what he would do to me. Suddenly, he hit me in the jaw with a karate chop. I heard my earring fly off, and I felt a crack in my jaw. I was afraid to touch my jaw because I was certain it was broken and didn't want to find out how badly. But, strangely enough, I didn't feel any pain. Chris turned and began walking towards the steps. As he passed a wall, he punched a hole in it. He was still carrying the broken tape. I followed him upstairs, anticipating he would attack my unsuspecting husband. He walked into our bedroom and began to speak calmly to Howie as if nothing happened. Then, again, he suddenly attacked Howie with a running side sick (a karate kick). As the psychologist instructed me, I told Chris I would have to call for an ambulance. At first Chris blew up. He started yelling, but he left our room and went into his bedroom. Only one minute later he emerged from his room, apparently much calmer, and apologized for what he had done and begged me not to call the hospital. When I checked my jaw, I was amazed to feel that it was fine. Without a doubt, God had protected me from injury. There was no way my jaw could have withstood such a blow from a strong teenager with a black belt in karate. He was capable of breaking several boards with one swift chop.

Having gone through an experience like that, you would imagine I would have gotten Chris into the hospital immediately because next time we might not be as fortunate. But there's no way to explain how difficult it is to commit your son to a psychiatric ward against his will. I knew ultimately it would be for his good, but I also knew initially it would be sheer agony. So I didn't call the hospital at that moment. I told Howie that if Chris did it again, we would have to call for an ambulance no matter what.

The very next night Chris assaulted us again. This time Chris hit Howie first and then me. When he turned his back to Howie to hit me (in the jaw again!), Howie got hold of him. I quickly left the room to call 911. But as I started walking downstairs, I thought, "What, are you nuts? How is Howie supposed to hold Chris down alone?" So I went back upstairs. As I entered our bedroom, I could see Howie was just losing his grip on Chris. If Chris got loose, there was no telling what damage he would do to us. When I entered the room, it distracted Chris enough for Howie to get a better hold on him. Quickly I helped Howie hold Chris down on the floor. I screamed to Robert to call 911 and ask for an ambulance. After Robert called for the ambulance, he hobbled into our bedroom to see if he could help. Robert had just gotten his cast off and so I didn't want him to help. I told him to just leave and close the door. I didn't want Robert to see us restraining our son, who sounded like an enraged animal.

We calculated later that it took at least ten minutes for the police to arrive. That was the longest ten minutes of my life. As we held Chris down on the floor, his nose started bleeding. Blood poured out of his nose and onto our carpet. Since Howie was on one side of Chris and I was on the other, I couldn't see what was happening. All I heard was Howie making grunting sounds as if he was getting hurt. Chris was head-butting Howie. Chris was trying to bite me. While we were wrestling him, somehow my finger got caught in his mouth. I had been trained that the correct thing to do was to jam my fist farther in to his mouth to release his grip. I did that and it worked! Shortly after, it happened again. He bit my hand and so I shoved my fist into his mouth. As I was removing my hand from his mouth, my baby finger got caught in the strong grips of his teeth. Just at that moment I heard a different sound from Howie. I heard him moan. I knew we had been exerting quite a bit of energy for such a long time under extreme emotionally upsetting conditions. I figured Howie's heart wasn't doing well. So I asked Howie, "Is it your heart?" He answered, "I think so." Later, I found out Robert heard all of what was going on and thought Howie was having a heart attack. As I looked at my finger in Chris's mouth, I considered my choices: I could leave it in so I could maintain my strong hold on

Chris, or I could move my other hand that was holding Chris to get my finger free. If I moved my other hand that was restraining Chris, he would surely get loose and hurt us both. If I didn't move my other hand, I honestly thought I was going to watch Chris bite my finger off!! I don't even remember what happened next. All I know is my finger was out of Chris's mouth and we both had a more secure hold on Chris. It was an eternity of silent agony.

An army of police officers came to our house. I never thought I would be relieved to have my son handcuffed, but I was. I knew that finally we would all be safe and Chris would have the best chance at getting better. I was exhausted and glad my work was over. The police took Chris away in an ambulance. As I quickly left the house to meet Chris at the hospital, I casually asked Robert if he wanted to come. When he responded, "Yes! I have to come; I've been traumatized!!" I realized my work wasn't over. Now I had to minister to Robert. As we drove to the hospital, the Lord helped me to speak calmly to Robert. I thanked him for what he had done, assuring him he had done the right thing. I explained what would be happening to Chris (without mentioning the gory details). I told him Chris would finally get the medication he needed to get better. Robert told me his stomach hurt him and he wouldn't be able to sleep. It was the only time I've ever seen him weepy as a teenager.

Anyone who has experienced the death of a loved one or gone through an extreme crisis would understand when I say that everything except my family seemed to be nonexistent (or nonimportant). For example, when we were at our house, I hadn't even noticed any of the police officers' faces. I hadn't noticed that our dog had messed on our steps. All I could focus on was my family. I certainly noticed Chris's face at the hospital. I arrived at the emergency area just on the heels of the ambulance and the police. As the police was escorting Chris into the hospital, I caught up with him. The empty look was gone from his eyes. Instead I saw the helpless, pleading eyes of a son who needed his mother. He said, "I'm sorry, Mom." I responded, "It's Okay, Chris. We know you didn't mean it.

You're just sick, that's all." The next thing I had to do was sit down at the admissions desk in the emergency room. Once again, I went through the motions without even noticing anyone around me. I started to get out my insurance cards. The nurse began asking me the routine questions as though this emergency was simply another routine emergency. "Patient's name?" she asked. And I answered. After a few more questions, she said in a different tone of voice, "You've done the hardest part, Mrs. Chandler, you got him here." I looked up at her face and noticed her caring eyes. How did she know what to say? How did she know what we had just done had been so incredibly hard? So I asked her, "How do you know that?" She answered, "I had to have my daughter admitted to this psychiatric unit recently." The Lord had given me another mother who understood what I was going through. I was able to ask her what she thought about the care and the program in that hospital. She assured me it was excellent.

From the hospital I called our pastors' emergency number. One of the youth pastors was on call. I asked him to come to the hospital to talk with Robert. In half an hour he arrived and talked with Robert for about an hour. After he left, Robert wanted to remain with us at the hospital, and was able to sleep there in the waiting room!

Once we got to the hospital, I was able to see the marks on Howie. The insides of his lips were raw and bloody from being hit repeatedly by Chris's head. There was a large cut on his face just under his eye. As I began to inspect myself I found no cuts, but I did find many bruises all over my arms and legs.

We wound up staying at the hospital for six hours. A crisis management person handled our case. It was his job to process the insurance information. He also had us try to get Chris to admit himself so that we wouldn't have to commit him against his will. He explained if we had to commit him against his will, we would have to have a hearing after a thorough evaluation was done to determine if he truly was incompetent. Chris was in a treatment room in the emergency room and we were in the waiting room. Several attempts to convince Chris to admit himself into the hospital resulted in his refusal each time. Finally, Chris fell asleep, so they took him directly to a room in the adolescent psychiatric ward of the hospital. God was gracious in providing a way for Chris to get treatment in a regular hospital so his peers wouldn't have to know exactly what was wrong with him. They simply knew he was sick and in the hospital. The hospital was only five minutes from our home, and our insurance covered every cent of the expenses (which turned out to be $25,000 for three weeks!).

As we left the hospital, we were given a packet of information about all the rules and regulations of the psychiatric ward. When we returned home, it was 6:00 AM. Robert got ready to go to bed. Howie began to clean up the dog's mess on the steps. As I entered our bedroom, I immediately noticed the pool of blood on our rug. I feverishly began scrubbing the rug before Robert saw it.

At one point Robert and I stood on the landing at the top of the stairs that connected all the bedrooms. Robert was standing near Chris's bedroom door that was mostly closed. He pointed to Chris's door and said to me, "He's in there." The past two months had prepared me to expect anything, so I assumed somehow Chris had escaped from the hospital. Still, with some disbelief, I peeked into Chris's room and caught a glimpse of legs in his bed. The shocked and puzzled look on my face told Robert I thought it was Chris in the room. Robert said, "It's Dad." As I pushed the door open I could see that Howie was lying in Chris's bed sobbing. I had never even seen Howie cry before, let alone sob! Once again, I realized my work wasn't over. I now had to minister to my husband. I went over to him to comfort him. All he said was, "It's all my fault. It's all my fault." I assured him Chris was simply sick mentally and would get better.

Robert quickly fell fast asleep. Before I attempted to sleep myself, I read all the information they had given us at the hospital. I knew it would be important for me to know what was going on with my son. There was no time for me to process or reflect on what had just happened. I knew Chris, Robert, and Howie would need me, and I needed to get some rest, if possible.

Later that day Howie and I compared notes. We shared what was going on in our minds as we held our son down waiting for the police to come and take him away to a psychiatric ward. We both felt tremendous sorrow for Chris. The Lord took that dreadful experience and helped me to see it in a beautiful way. Howie and I were careful not to hurt Chris as we held him down. Neither of us minded the blows he gave us. Even though he cursed us, we loved him unconditionally because we understood. That's just how it is with Jesus. He died for us because he loves us unconditionally. He was wounded for our transgressions. No matter how much we curse Him or stray from Him, He loves us just the same because he understands us.

A few hours after we got home, I received a call from the hospital to tell me Chris was refusing medication. They were calling for permission to give it to him as an injection. I gave my permission. When I called later, I found out Chris had been put in isolation because he had put up such a fight when they tried to give him the medication. I had to fight back the mental images of my son sedated, confused, and in an isolation room. They said I could come to visit Chris because they were about to take him out of isolation anyway (since the medication would be sedating him).

When I got to the hospital, I was hit with the reality of it. The psychiatric unit was locked. In order to gain entrance I had to ring a bell and announce who I was. Then a nurse came to let me in. The information I had read explained that guests (even family members) have to visit the patients in lounge areas (rather than in their bedrooms). But as I walked down the hall of the unit for the first time, I was ushered into Chris's room. There sat a woman who didn't introduce herself to me. She had been talking with Chris. It was a very sensitive moment for Chris and for me because that was the first time we had seen each other since the terrible scene at home, and since we had him committed there. It was the first time I saw Chris, who looked so sedated and emotionally broken. Even though he was on heavy doses of medication and psychotic, Chris apologized to me. I told him there was no need for apology because I understood he was just sick. The strange woman started asking me some questions, intruding on our private moment. I asked her who she was and she explained she was Chris's psychiatrist! She still didn't even give me her name. She told me Chris was contradicting himself. I told her that of course he was contradicting himself; he was psychotic!!! I began to question her. I asked her why she was in his bedroom and why she allowed me to be in his bedroom. She informed me she had just started working in that hospital and wasn't familiar with the procedures of the ward. I thought to myself, if I was able to read the information during my crisis, why wasn't she able to prepare herself for her job?!! I wondered if she was even qualified at all!! Later that day I typed a letter to the chief psychiatrist requesting Chris have a different psychiatrist. Chris was then switched to the care of the head psychiatrist.

While at the hospital, Chris had to be strip-searched; he was included with troubled teens (who were either suicidal, drug abusers, or violent); he had to get a nurse to unlock his bathroom when he needed to use it; all his belongings were taken from him; and there were very strict rules (about when he could call us, what he could wear and what belongings he could have). Even his clothes were misplaced because Chris put them in the laundry bin in which the other patients put their hospital gowns. But the hospital gowns were sent away to be cleaned. I couldn't understand how the nurses expected Chris to be responsible for his own dirty laundry while psychotic and on heavy doses of medication. It's no wonder Chris literally thought he was in jail. He had to experience all this while mentally ill and on Haldol. It was so hard for me to witness him desperately trying to figure out what he had to do to get released from there. It was obvious he felt like he was being punished for hitting us.

After I met Chris's new psychiatrist, I felt more relieved. He actually listened to me about my concerns regarding the medication Chris was on. I explained the importance of keeping him off any stimulants or antidepressants, as they could exacerbate his ADHD and cause his Tourrette Syndrome to become worse. The psychiatrist took him off Haldol and put him on a psychotropic medication called Trillifon (for psychosis). He also prescribed Depakote for Chris's hypomania (mild mood swings). Chris also had to take Cogentin to prevent tardive dyskinesia (rigidity that sometimes results from taking psychotropic medications).

Howie and I visited Chris every time there were visiting hours and we stayed the whole time. Sadly, none of the other patients had such faithful visitors. Chris began to appreciate our unconditional love for him. When we were in the hospital visiting, Chris begged us to get him out of there. He would lay his head in my lap and ask me to stroke him. When my boys grew up I had missed doing things like that. It was bittersweet to be able to nurture Chris, who was a young man, in that way. I was happy to be able to comfort him, but it ate me up inside to see him so pathetic, so broken. Howie passed the time by playing cards or chess with Chris. Robert didn't want to see his brother in such a place. For a while I respected that. I knew Robert was dealing with lots of questions from curious (some caring and some nosy) students at school. He was also struggling with getting around school on crutches. But finally I asked Robert to visit Chris because he needed to see his brother, his friend. It hurt me to have to force Robert to see his brother in the hospital. Robert, being very compliant, agreed to go. When Robert visited, he played chess with Chris. Chris beat Robert. I whispered to Robert, "Did you let him win?" Robert whispered back, "No....It's like the movie 'Phenomenon.' Chris seems to have more skill."

During the time Chris was in the hospital, there were several things that were hard to hear. For example, one day when I was talking on the phone to Chris, he told me he thought it was a good plan of mine to put him in the hospital to see that life can be even worse than he ever imagined. Another day Chris told me one of his fellow patients knew one of the girls in Chris's marching band. When that fellow patient called the girl from the hospital, he told the girl Chris was there too. At that moment I knew everyone in school would find out what was going on with Chris. I knew I couldn't protect him from gossip. Even though I understood that mental illness is simply an illness and shouldn't be perceived as a character flaw, I knew most people don't see it that way. One of my worst fears was that one day someone at school might say to Chris something like, "Hey, I heard you're nuts!" One student actually did say that to Robert. At lunch one day he asked Robert, "Is your brother crazy?!" Quickly, one of Robert's (Christian) friends answered, "No! You're the crazy one!!"

It came time for the hearing. I had lost a lot of weight because I was found to be glucose intolerant (borderline diabetic). The doctor had put me on the "Fen-Phen" diet. I had lost 50 pounds in six months. Since I had been at home with Chris for so long, I didn't have anything to wear except jeans. I had to get something to wear to the hearing. I pondered, what does one wear to a hearing against her own son? The saleslady at the local Dress Barn recognized me and commented on how good I looked since I had lost so much weight. None of that mattered to me. I couldn't even enjoy my new figure. I discovered there were levels of a mother's sadness. Mild sadness is cured by a good dose of chocolate. Prayer can cure moderate sadness. Then there's the extreme sadness and sorrow I experienced when Chris was in kindergarten and I learned what it meant to 'cry out' to the Lord. When Chris was in the hospital, however, I discovered a deeper sadness that even strips you of any appetite. It's a sadness that prevents you even from talking. Crying doesn't help either because there aren't enough tears to soothe the pain. When my pastor saw me he let me know he understood the depth of my pain by saying, "You're not on the 'Fen-Phen' diet. You're on the Chris-Chris diet, aren't you?" The only comfort a mother can find with that kind of sorrow is by staying in God's Word. So that's what I did.

For the hearing Chris was assigned a lawyer from Social Services. There was a lawyer for the hospital. We were not provided a lawyer, but were told we could arrange to have one on our own. We didn't get one. The lawyer for the hospital was kind enough to explain to us what was going to happen. He said Chris would be asked if he would agree to remain in the hospital. If he did not agree, then we would have to go to court. If that happened, witnesses would have to be brought in (including the police who came to our house and possibly even Robert!). He pointed out that in all likelihood Chris would lose the court case, so it was in his best interest to agree to remain in the hospital. I couldn't imagine how Chris would understand all that in the condition he was in. Even if he was clear-headed and not on any medication, I couldn't imagine him agreeing to remain in such a place. It wasn't a chamber of horrors, but being in the hospital is normally no fun, and it's even worse when there are so many rules and strict procedures. He told us we could talk with Chris briefly prior to the hearing. As we explained the situation to Chris, he struggled to understand it. He desperately wanted to do the right thing, and yet he desperately wanted to get out of that hospital. Miraculously he agreed to say he wanted to remain in the hospital. That was only the first step. He had to repeat that to the judge at the hearing.

We were ushered into a room. Howie and I were seated behind Chris (not even at the table with the others!). Chris was seated next to his lawyer. There were so many moments over the last few months I just couldn't believe were happening, and that was one of them. How we loved Chris and ached for him! He looked so vulnerable and helpless in that place. He had to sit there and hear the official report from the psychiatrist about what he had done and about what was wrong with him. Then the judge asked him the all-important question. Chris hesitated, struggling to remember what to say through his confused state and his medication. At last he agreed to remain in the hospital. I was so proud of him. I was so thankful and yet sad he had to continue to endure being in the hospital.

Part of Chris's therapy at the hospital required him to tell several people every day why he was in the hospital. Every day Chris had to tell the nurses what he had done to us. I just didn't understand why he had to repeat that over and over again. I could understand why the other teenagers in the ward would have to repeat what they had done (attempted suicide, drug abuse, and willful violence). It would have made more sense to have Chris explain that he had resisted medication for his illness during the two months prior to his hospitalization. He had to spend hours of therapy where they talked about drug abuse, eating disorders, and suicide. What he really needed was hours of therapy discussing how to handle rejection from peers, and the pain and anger that resulted from that.

But Chris was smart enough to figure out what he had to do to get out of the hospital. So he regularly told the staff he had assaulted his parents. After three weeks it was time for him to be released. I had never cleaned the house so thoroughly! I wanted his room and his bathroom and our home to look the best it could for him. We were so thankful to have our son home again!

Chapter 11
"You're Over-involved, Mrs. Chandler."

Finally, Chris was released from residential treatment (in the hospital) and placed in a partial-care program. He went to a psychiatric facility for about six hours during the day and stayed home for the rest of the day and at night. The social worker at the hospital had worked very hard to find a good "match" for Chris. She wanted to find a facility that would be covered by our insurance, that wouldn't be too far from our home, and that wouldn't have too many patients.

Another very difficult day during this trial was when I had to leave Chris at his partial-care facility for the first time. Many parents find it difficult to leave their children at a new school for the first day in the fall. I've even seen a mother of a middle school girl crying because she couldn't manage to leave her daughter at a new school. You can just imagine how hard it was for me to trust my confused, hurting son with perfect strangers. I drove home wondering why no one was there to help me through that hurdle in the process. It was all part of my learning experience that there are no organized support systems for the families of those who are mentally ill (outside of the church and family).

The main building of the facility had recently had a fire so Chris and all the other patients had to spend the six hours each day in a small trailer. Chris couldn't stand it because he felt closed in. It reminded him too much of the adolescent psychiatric unit at the hospital from which he had just been released. He said he felt like a caged animal.

When I picked him up after his first day, Chris said the social worker assigned to him spoke meanly to him. It was hard to ascertain if that really was true or not. But when I met his social worker, she told me she was pregnant, unhappy in her job, and looking for a different profession!

On Chris's second day in that program, he met his psychiatrist and they spoke for less than 30 minutes. When I picked Chris up he seemed extremely unhappy. My intuition told me his reaction was based on a bad situation, rather than on his condition. His medication had started to really help him return to the "old Chris." I decided to let Chris stay home the next day (to take a break from the program). I didn't know that according to Chris's school district's policy, it wasn't allowed. Since Chris was supposed to be in the partial-care program, he was expected to be there every day. I called the guidance counselor at Chris's school to discuss the details of the homebound instruction Chris would need, and that's when I found out one of the social workers was very upset with me.

I called that social worker and she proceeded to yell at me, saying I was too over-involved. She informed me the psychiatrist at the partial care facility called them to say Chris was ready to go back to school. He made that determination without having read Chris's hospital records or spoken to his hospital psychiatrist or me! He came to that conclusion based on his brief conversation with Chris. The social worker apparently thought I was trying to keep Chris home so he could play hooky from school (even though they had a written diagnosis and excuse note from Chris's outpatient psychiatrist). Once again, the Lord helped me to respond correctly. I made it clear to her that, as far as I was concerned, there was no way I could ever be "over-involved" with my son. I went on to point out that since I was the one in crisis and she was supposedly the professional, she should begin speaking to me with more compassion. I clarified how the psychiatrist at the partial-care facility made his determination based on insufficient information. I explained that the social worker at the partial-care facility openly admitted she didn't like her job, and therefore, wasn't invested in doing what was needed to be done for my son. So I kept him home for one day where he would be cared for properly. I told her if there were some sort of procedure to follow, I'd be happy to follow it. But in lieu of anyone taking the lead, I would do it. She explained it was the responsibility of the social worker at the partial-care facility to arrange a meeting with all their staff, the school district's Director of Student Services, Chris, and us. She offered to encourage that social worker to arrange for the meeting as soon as possible.

Chris started going to some band rehearsals after school. One night there was a performance. I was very concerned about how he would handle the pressure, and wondered if he would act normally in front of everyone. As I sat in the auditorium waiting for the program to begin, I wondered where Chris was and what he was doing backstage. I couldn't be with him. I hoped he wouldn't do or say anything to embarrass himself or Robert. Since he had been absent for so long, many of the other students would be asking him questions. We had rehearsed what he'd say. We told him to respond simply by saying, "I was sick and now I'm feeling better." While I sat there lost in thought, another band parent came over to me. It was a parent I didn't know well. With not one ounce of sensitivity, she asked me what I thought of the partial-care facility Chris attended. I was shocked she knew and that she was so rude to mention it to me. I asked her how she knew Chris was receiving care there. She told me a friend of hers had a daughter who was also there with Chris. Great! Just perfect!! I figured everyone knew our business, and realized it would be impossible to keep Chris's friends from finding out. I can't believe I actually answered her intrusive question, instead of politely telling her she shouldn't have asked me. It was just one more indication that people do not understand how upsetting it is to have a loved one who is mentally ill. If nothing else, it would have been nice to have enjoyed the band performance without having someone remind me that Chris was recovering from his illness.

When I was taking Chris home from the partial-care facility one day, he was telling me once again how bad it was there. The three months of stress had taken its toll on me. In sheer frustration, I lost my temper with Chris and spoke harshly to him. Later, I felt tremendous guilt and I felt like a failure. I couldn't allow myself to wallow in self-pity, so I asked Chris's out-patient psychologist to give me some feedback on how I had been handling the situation. He assured me I had handled it amazingly well considering the circumstances, and had persevered for a long time. He told me I needed to take time out for myself (to get rest and relaxation). He encouraged me to find some time for entertainment for myself.

There was one day I'll cherish in the midst of those difficult days. Chris and I spent some time walking by a creek together. When I was younger I used to sit for hours on a rock in a creek near our house. I marveled at God's creation. When I was surrounded by God's creation instead of the world (man-made things, and earthly troubles) I found peace (even though I hadn't yet accepted the Lord as my Savior). It was comforting to see God's power and love demonstrated in his beautiful creation. As I walked by the creek with Chris I pointed out the water. I shared with him what I often thought of when I was younger. The calm water was nice. As long as it was perfectly still it could reflect the most sunlight. But even the water that rippled over the rocks glistened in the sunlight. It was the turbulence in the water that made the soothing sounds and caused the brightest sparkling light. Then I compared it to our lives. When things are going smoothly in our lives, we can reflect God's love as long as we remain perfectly still - yielded to Him. But even when turbulence comes into our lives we can also reflect his love in a more vibrant way. The lesson was that God could be glorified the most through our trials. Then I finished the analogy by pointing out there is still water before and after the turbulent water. I assured him his life would once again become calm - that God would help him pass through the turbulent times and the current trial would end.

Chapter 12
Out of the Crisis, But It's Not Over

Thankfully, we found a combination of drugs that seemed to help Chris think and feel normally. Chris returned to out-patient therapy (regularly seeing his Christian psychologist and his psychiatrist). Chris was ready to begin making up the work he had missed while out of school for two months. I couldn't imagine how he (or anyone) could make up all that work and at the same time begin going back to school. Chris desperately wanted to get back to school; he just wanted his life restored and to feel normal again. He needed tutors who could help him make up the work from his honors pre-calculus class, his honors physics class, his honors German III class, and his Advanced Placement English Literature course. Amazingly, the Lord provided perfectly for those needs. He had three different tutors. One homebound instructor was his own German teacher. Another was the husband of one of the teachers at my school. He taught honors physics in another public school, so Chris had a Christian man who was well equipped to teach him his physics and his pre-calculus. His third tutor was formerly the superintendent of his district who had his doctorate in English. He helped Chris with his English Literature course.

Chris was gradually weaned back to school, starting first with only one or two days a week at school and building up to a full week. He even went to the practices for all the four bands he was in (orchestra, wind ensemble, jazz band, and marching band). Knowing that there is healing and encouragement in God's Word, I sent Chris to school with a Bible verse on a card to keep in his pocket. I wasn't sure whether he would even look at it, but I felt it was worth a try. I needed to somehow teach Chris how to walk with the Lord himself.

Chris had made so much progress, but he needed to learn how to prevent difficulties in the future. His psychologist and psychiatrist were extremely helpful in providing practical suggestions for Chris. They discussed with him ways to avoid stressful situations, how to set realistic goals for himself, how to seek help when needed, and how to "renew his mind." Dr. Kipley gave him a very simple, yet profound formula that Chris was supposed to follow any time he had some negative feelings. He was to answer the following questions:

1) What are my negative feelings?
2) What is the situation?
3) What is my negative self-talk? (usually all negative)
4) What is the lie?
5) What is the truth? (mostly positive, and sometimes a little negative)

In our Christian counseling it was healing for all of us to hear that God wants us to experience joy and to have an abundant life.

Over the past few months I had seen God's love toward us demonstrated in so many ways. Chris, however, still couldn't see how much healing had taken place because he was still recovering and busy making up work. Chris still felt at times that God didn't love him (since God had allowed his life to be shattered). My desire was that Chris would be able to see that God really did love him, had healed him, and could answer very specific prayers in his life. So I asked God to reveal the healing and His love to Chris. Since it is God's good pleasure to demonstrate His love to us, He answered that prayer in several amazing ways.

Students had to audition to be in the jazz band at Chris's school. The director selected music played by professional musicians, and the jazz band participated in some of the local competitions. Chris hadn't practiced his trombone at all at home; he only went to practices. One day they were doing a performance for about 150 senior citizens at a nursing home. One of the other trombone players in the band didn't show up. That other musician had two critical solos. Without him there, the director turned to Chris (as they were walking on the stage!) and asked him to play the other part. Chris agreed, and proceeded to sight-read the other part perfectly - in front of the audience. He then spontaneously created an improvisation solo that would fit the background music for the missing student's other solo. His fellow musicians were stunned to witness what Chris was able to do, and they didn't even know that he was just recovering from an illness that affected his mind.

Another way God revealed his love and healing to Chris was when he took several pre-calculus tests in 10 days. Chris had to make up two tests and take a test that was currently being given to all the students. On one of the make-up tests there was a problem none of the other students had gotten correct, but Chris got it correct! The most amazing testimony of God's healing power in Chris's life was when the school year ended and Chris had made up all his work on time and earned nothing lower than a B on his report card for the entire year.

Whenever a family goes through a significant crisis, it's never completely over when it's over. Howie and I found we were unusually tired. In addition, I found I cried easily (I thought because I was so full of joy that Chris was better). I asked Dr. Kipley if what we were experiencing was normal, considering what we had been through, and he said it was.

One day I found myself overreacting to a situation. Robert had called and asked me to pick him up after school. When I got to the school I saw no signs of Robert. As I waited in the car I observed a huge crowd of high school students walking just off the school grounds (out of my sight). Then I saw the principal and vice principal walk to that area. Shortly after, I saw the huge crowd dispersing and the principal and vice principal return to the school building. It appeared that "something was going down" - perhaps a fight. My suspicions were correct because then I saw two police cars arrive. All the while, I was wondering where Robert was. Had he not just called me for a ride, I would have thought I had the wrong day. But he had just phoned for me to come get him. I started worrying Robert was the one that was the target of some sort of violence. With the way our lives were going, I figured Robert probably was getting beat up!

Then I told myself to just calm down, maybe he's just watching the whole thing. With that thought in my mind, I decided I'd personally kill him for being even an observer of such a thing!! Finally, I drove to a pay phone to call home. Robert answered the phone! As teenagers typically do (just to make life miserable for their parents!), he had simply changed his mind and caught a ride home with someone else.

I was ready to fall apart. Now that I knew Robert was safe, I was relieved. It was time to have a good cry. As I drove away from the school I noticed a police car was right behind me. Well, that good cry would just have to wait; I had to concentrate on my speed and maintain 15 miles an hour. Do you know how hard that is? I had never noticed the road leading off school grounds was so long. Finally, I turned onto the road that borders the school property (a 25-mile-an-hour speed limit). Still shaken, I stopped paying attention to my rear view mirror. When I got to the first light, I turned left and noticed the police car was also making a left turn. The road we turned on to had two lanes in each direction. I slowed down so the police officer would pass me, but he didn't. I really didn't need this. I was trying to either fall apart of calm down (I hadn't decided which!). After passing about three more lights, the police car was still behind me. At last I arrived at the industrial park where I turn to take a short cut home. I made a right-hand turn and the police officer followed me. Then he put his lights on to pull me over. Perfect, just perfect!!

I had never been pulled over by a police officer before. I got out the appropriate documents (license, registration, etc.) and waited. As I looked in my rear view mirror, I could see the officer just sitting in his car. What was going on? I began to think all kinds of things. Maybe he thought I was a high school student that was somehow involved in the fight. Maybe he was waiting for more back-up. Oh, how embarrassing! I couldn't imagine what I had done wrong. I decided to tell him the truth: my son was missing and I thought he was being beaten up. The officer would believe me because he had just followed me all the way from the high school. I waited so long I began to wonder if I was supposed to get out of my car and go to him.

Finally, the police officer got out of his car and walked to my car. As he approached my window he said, "Hi! How are you doing?" in a very pointed manner. I figured he must be interested in how I was doing since I had a fairly short skirt on. Obviously, I wasn't thinking clearly. He told me I needed to get the registration sticker on my car. It was April and the sticker should have been put on in January. It's no wonder why Howie had neglected to remember that little detail with everything else that was going on in our lives.

Even though the officer was simply giving me a reminder to get the sticker on and wasn't asking me any questions, I felt the need to unload on him emotionally. So, I proceeded to tell him my son was just missing. He asked me if I knew where he was, and I told him I knew he was home. Then the officer added that he knew my son. I was instantly back on my emotional roller coaster. Why would a local police officer know my son?!! I was back to thinking, "I'll kill him, myself!" As casually as I could say the words, I asked, "Oh? How do you know my son?" The officer said, "I was there that night." I knew exactly what he meant by "that night;" he was referring to when we had to call for an ambulance to take Chris to the hospital to have him committed.

All of a sudden the emotions of that night flooded my heart like a tidal wave. I remembered that Chris, in his distorted thinking, had accused Howie and me of doing to him what he had done to us. Chris later explained that he did that so the police wouldn't take him to jail. He had accused us of assaulting him, of physically abusing him, and I never knew what the police believed. They didn't know us. And now, I was face to face with one of those officers.

Before I could speak, the officer asked, "How is your son doing?" I answered that he was doing fine. Then I got my wits about me and told him it was a shame he had seen Chris like that because it wasn't at all like our son. The officer said he knew that it was obvious. He even said Chris was "pretty funny" that night. Well, "pretty funny" wasn't how I'd ever describe him, but it was clear the officer knew exactly what was going on at the time. As I drove away, the officer was still behind me. Was he going to follow me home? But he didn't. As I replayed that last scene in the sequence of upsetting events (the fight, being pulled over, the police officer knowing my son, the police officer being there "that night"), I realized when the officer first approached my car window and asked me how I was doing, he really was concerned about how I was doing (since the incident). I'm sure when he was having my car checked to see if it was registered, he recognized the name and address.

At times there were hints of Chris's sense of humor. Sometimes it came out at very unexpected times. I was attending one of the many concerts Chris and Robert were in as part of the Spring Arts Festival in the school district. Since the boys were in several bands, they went on and off stage several times throughout the night. One time I watched Chris's band filing into the auditorium to sit in the seats between their performances. A chorus was about to perform, but they hadn't all gotten on the risers. Chris was the very last member of his band to enter the auditorium. He hesitated and then went back out. Then I saw him letting one last member of his band into the auditorium. Suddenly I saw one of the directors pull Chris back out of the auditorium. She apparently thought Chris was disrupting the performance, but it hadn't started yet. She obviously didn't realize Chris was just being thoughtful to let a straggler into the auditorium. I knew the Lord knew his heart. Since I couldn't comfort Chris myself, I prayed the Lord would speak to Chris so he would feel His assurance more than hear that director's angry words. Later that night at home we talked about what had happened. Chris was upset that the director got angry with him. I asked if Chris had heard God's still small voice letting him know He knew Chris's intentions. Chris responded, "Yea, Mom. I heard voices" and he smiled a teasing smile. It was good to see Chris could tease about something like that.

As Chris returned to school, I returned to work. It was good to be back at my school surrounded by so many understanding and supportive friends. Bill was allowing me to come and go as I needed. He made it clear to me that if Chris needed me I should be with him. At work it was sometimes difficult dealing with certain situations. I found I had less patience with parents who made a big deal out of what I perceived as trivial problems. Compared to what we just lived through, an F on a test didn't seem like such a big deal in all of eternity. But it still was my job to help teachers deal with parents who were strung out about one low test grade as though it were some major crisis. I had to remind myself that any time a parent is concerned about their child, strong feelings are involved. If a parent has to see their child unhappy, that's upsetting to the parent. Even though to me an F as a final grade wouldn't be the end of the world, I had to remember that an F would be upsetting to any parent who hasn't experienced a life-changing, priority-changing crisis with a child. It seemed like I was encountering several parents who were going through a similar experience. At first I thought that I was simply trying to find mental illness under every bush, now that I was much more aware of it. But then I realized that the Lord was already using me to minister to others. I found opportunities to share the comfort and hope that I had found in the Lord.

In talking to other parents who had children suffering from mental illness, I began to see a pattern. Most of the parents indicated they couldn't get their teenagers to agree to speak to a psychologist or psychiatrist. I remembered that when I was a teenager, I had been extremely depressed for a while and I didn't want to talk to anyone, let alone a professional who would want to pry into my emotions. I began to appreciate Chris's determination even more.

That spring I went to a women's retreat. It was wonderful to get away from the whole ordeal and just fellowship with other women. The theme of the retreat was that Jesus is the Potter and we are the clay (being molded into vessels worthy of service for Him). On the last day of the retreat one of the speakers held up a beautiful and expensive cup and saucer she said was very special to her. She explained it was special to her because a friend had given it to her as a gift for journeying with her from insanity to sanity. I was struck by the way she lovingly said, "journeying from insanity to sanity" and yet the painful, empty feeling returned to the pit of my stomach. She asked all those who wanted to be servants of God, to be vessels chosen by the Master Potter, to stand. Well, just about all 500 women in attendance rose simultaneously. The entire weekend had been so inspiring. But I just stayed planted firmly in my seat, thinking, "Oh, no...I know what this is all about. I've just been through the fire. Now I'll be content to let the Lord just leave me on the shelf for a while!" My thoughts were interrupted by the realization of how this must look. Miss Christian School Administrator not willing to be God's servant. But, I didn't care. I wasn't going to stand to be seen of men...I mean to be seen of women. But then I started thinking about how much I had seen God work in our lives through it all. The words from one of the workshops that weekend echoed in my mind. "The deeper the pit, the brighter the light." Surely, the trial had been bittersweet. I had experienced the provision and comfort of God, first hand. So, then I stood confidently with tears rolling down my face, willing to smile at the future if God chose to use me and remold me once again. I knew no matter what I would face in the future, I'd be okay because I'm a child of the King.

Chapter 13
A Temporary Oasis

The summer after Chris's junior year we went to Colorado. It was wonderful. It was as if nothing had ever gone wrong and Chris hadn't been sick at all. We had a fantastic time horseback riding, visiting with my brother and his family, hiking, "panning" for gold, and mountain biking. We were all very relaxed except for when Robert really did get lost for a brief time taking a wrong turn biking down a mountain in Vail.

Also during the summer Chris and Robert went to the same college for a few days for music workshops. Chris went to a band leadership training camp with about 500 band leaders (mostly all drum majors). He had attended the training the year before. But this year it would be quite different. This was the first time he had to take his medication on his own. I knew it would be a temptation for him to just not take his medication. But I knew it was important for him to see I trusted him to be responsible. I knew Robert would be at the same college, but they would be staying at different dorms. Robert was attending a percussion camp. Thankfully, Chris handled another major step in his recovery quite well. He knew he could handle being away from home and he could be responsible enough to take his medication.

Chris had hoped one day he would be the drum major of his marching band. He had a good chance to accomplish that goal until he got sick. Even after he was sick, he still had all the necessary qualities of a good drum major: excellent music abilities, remarkable marching abilities, and strong leadership skills (his peers didn't embrace him as a friend, but they did respect him). When Chris had his breakdown, not only was his life temporarily shattered, but his dreams of becoming a drum major were shattered as well. But yet, there he was at the band leadership training camp surrounded by drum majors. I was so proud of his resilience and his ability to take risks in life.

During the leadership training there is a march off. That's kind of like "Simon Says" only with someone calling out marching commands. If someone carries out a command incorrectly, he is eliminated. The competition continues until there is one winner remaining. Out of 500 drum majors Chris lasted until the last six. Only five others remained longer than he did. Once again, God blessed him by letting him see that he still had it.

Chris was a squad leader for the marching band again. I marveled at how clear thinking he was as he planned for his meetings with his squad members. He thought of everything: to offer rides to our house, to plan the refreshments, to prepare the agenda, to have the newest members arrive earlier than the veteran members, etc. One day he asked me for a suggestion of something nice he could do for the freshman band members. I asked him to think of something an upperclassman had done for him. Chris said when he was a freshman, a senior band member invited Chris to go out for pizza with some other senior band members. That made Chris feel very special. Soon after that conversation I found Chris organizing a huge pizza lunch at a local restaurant for all the freshman and senior band members. It was very thoughtful and quite an undertaking. But Chris managed it all!!

With Chris's senior year fast approaching, we spent some days in the summer visiting colleges. Sometimes I wanted to continue on with our plans as though nothing had happened. But then I had to force myself to remember that something significant did happen. We had to pray for wisdom to know which colleges to investigate. As usual, Chris was very clear in what he wanted, and his decisions made perfect sense. He wanted to go to a college with a fairly small campus that was about an hour and a half away from home (far enough to live away from home, but yet still close enough to visit home frequently). He also wanted a state university because that would be more affordable. He especially was interested in Penn State because of their famous "Blue Band" he hoped to join in his junior year of college. He was also interested in Penn State because they have an excellent business program. Chris's plans are to major in business because he wants to become an actuary. So Chris applied to Kutztown State University and Penn State University (Berks campus). By October he had been accepted to both colleges. That just confirmed two things I knew: people with mental illness can lead happy and successful lives, and we serve an awesome God!

During three weeks in the fall we hosted a German exchange student. It was a wonderful experience for all of us. We did many special things as a family every weekend, such as visiting local tourist sites.

In the fall Chris got his driver's license. He had a fear he would get in a car accident. My concern was if he got into a car accident, he might not be able to handle it emotionally. Being in a car accident is upsetting enough for anyone who hasn't gone through what he had recently been through. If I were God, I would make sure Chris would never have a car accident. But, thank goodness I'm not God. God saw fit to have Chris face his fears. Chris was in a minor accident. There were no injuries and Chris hadn't broken any laws, so he didn't get a ticket either. There was plenty of damage, but Chris was fine emotionally. He wasn't eager to drive after that, but he seemed to be reacting to it just about how any teenager would react.

Speaking of teenagers — we did have two teenagers in our family. For many parents, that alone is a major crisis in life. Thankfully, the most problems we encountered were with Robert — that he was girl crazy. One day Howie bought Robert a T-shirt that had an interactive drum set on it. If you touched a drum or a cymbal a sound would come from his shirt. When I saw it, I thought I would love to have one for my "joy box" collection. That was just the kind of thing I would love. When I picked Robert up from school the day he wore it, I asked him what everyone thought about his shirt (thinking all his band buddies probably loved it). He said all the girls wanted to "play" his shirt all day. Then he said with a grin, "Too many girls, such little time." The next day in school I shared his comment with Bill (who really understood teenagers). Bill asked me, "What were you thinking when you saw him wearing that shirt!" I responded, "I was thinking I wanted one for myself!"

Sometimes Robert's social life would seem to close in on him. We have call waiting on our phone. One time while he was on the phone with one girl, the girl had to put him on hold while she got call waiting from another girl that Robert talks to regularly on the phone. Then Robert got a call waiting signal and it was a third girl that Robert speaks to on the phone regularly. He kept telling us the girls really wouldn't mind. He also took three different girls to see the movie "Titanic" on three different occasions. One time he took one of them to see the movie on a Sunday afternoon. He asked us to drop her off at her church straight after the movies so she could get to her youth night on time. When he got home he started to chuckle. He told us he just realized that the girl he took to see "Titanic" the first time also attended that youth group. It was completely feasible for the second girl to happen to mention she had just seen the movie with Robert, and then the first girl would inform her she had already see the same movie with Robert too.

Aside from that, Robert was well liked and respected by his peers and teachers. He was also an honors student getting all A's and B's. He was solid in his faith, even though he attended public school, usually finding Christian friends (male and female!). So aside from Chris's little breakdown, the teenage years with our boys weren't too bad!

During this time when Chris was feeling better he was able to explain what it was like to be paranoid, and to be on Haldol. It was amazing how creative he was in describing what he experienced. He told me when he was paranoid he "hung onto one particular part of what someone was saying" and focused on just that. According to Chris, being on Haldol was like having his body frozen or moving in slow motion, while his brain was moving at a much faster pace.

When it came time for County and District Band auditions, Chris wanted to try out again. The year before, that was the "straw that broke the camel's back." But how could I tell him he couldn't audition? He was a musician. If I told him he couldn't try out, he would think I was trying to control him and treat him like a child. He also would think I didn't think he could handle it, and he would feel like he was flawed. But what if he tried out and "lost it" again? Soon, our "oasis" would be gone.

Chapter 14
Here We Go Again

The only thing worse than watching your son "lose his mind" was noticing some warning signs that indicated it was about to happen again. During Chris's senior year in high school that's exactly what happened to me twice. We had learned quite a bit the first time around, but there was still a lot for me to learn. When I realized Chris was close to the edge again, I felt very helpless because I didn't know anything could be done. At the same time, I felt confident the Lord would sustain me as He had before. But I was dreading having to watch Chris suffer like that again. I wasn't sure what the Lord would allow this time.

Typically, students who struggle emotionally or academically have the most problems in October and in March because those are the months with the fewest breaks during the school year. Chris was no exception. He had a "mini-crisis" at both those times. Each time we were able to prevent another breakdown because, once I noticed the warning signs, I got his psychiatrist and psychologist involved immediately. Chris had excellent psychiatric help, and we were very aggressive with the treatments.

Shortly after our German exchange student left I noticed Chris wasn't smiling at all. When I picked him up after school - especially after he had band practice — he acted differently than normal. He was either extremely talkative or he fell asleep immediately in the car. He started getting some nose bleeds, which indicated his blood pressure might have been unusually high again. I knew we had to do something, but I worried there was nothing that could be done about it. Looking back, I feel ashamed I wasted emotional energy worrying. God tells us in His Word we shouldn't be anxious because it can't add one day to our lives. In my mind I know worrying doesn't accomplish anything (except maybe health problems if we worry often enough!). In my heart I believe God is able to do beyond all that we imagine. But, yet, I worried the situation would only get worse.

When we took Chris to see his Christian psychiatrist, Dr. Newman, we learned there was a very simple solution we could try. Dr. Newman explained we could give him a tiny bit of extra medication at the time of the day when he experienced the most stress. Initially, that made no sense to me because most of his medications caused him to be drowsy. And with him sleeping more as it was, I thought giving him more medication would just make him sleep more. But Dr. Newman explained when Chris experienced additional stress, his brain produced adrenaline. The adrenaline, being a chemical, reduced the effectiveness of his medication for his psychosis. It made his mind race so he could perform under the stressful conditions. That's why he was more talkative when he first got in the car with me after school. Then, once the stressful condition (band practice) was over, Chris would experience a "bounce" which Dr. Newman described as a sharp decline in his mental energy. That's why he fell asleep so suddenly. It was a way his body allowed him to recover from the stressful experience. Many parents see this type of thing happen with infants when they experience stress. For example, when babies have to get an injection they cry a lot and then fall asleep after the ordeal is over (the sharp decline in mental energy following a stressful experience).

So, we agreed to try administering just a tiny bit of that medication "as needed" — at just the right time of day. I was still worried. I thought it could be dangerous to increase the dosage of a psycotropic medication with a teenager who was on the brink of another breakdown. I asked Dr. Neman what could happen if it didn't work. Could it bring on a psychotic episode? Dr. Newman didn't really answer my question. All he said was, "That would be a 'mini-crisis' and you should beep me and say that it's an emergency."

Since Chris was the one who could determine when he was experiencing increased stress, he had to be the one to administer his extra pill. I knew Chris wouldn't go to the nurse to get his extra pill if he needed it. Going to the nurse's office might make him late for band practice. Being late for band practice would just add more stress on top of extra stress. I also knew Chris wouldn't appreciate having the nurse show up at band practice to give him his extra pill. In addition, I knew that in our nation, educators have mounted a "zero tolerance" policy in the schools against drugs. Students who are found carrying even over-the-counter medication can be suspended. But, thankfully, I was familiar with the American with Disabilities Act (the ADA) which requires that "reasonable accommodations" be made for individuals with disabilities. Chris certainly had a disability, and so the school was obligated by law to allow a "reasonable accommodation." (See Part Two for more information about the ADA.)

My plan was to call the nurse and simply request that Chris be allowed to administer his own extra pill as needed. I didn't want to come on strong about his rights if it wasn't necessary. So I began by giving the nurse the opportunity to agree the best way to handle the situation would be to let Chris carry the pill in his pocket, with a note from the nurse explaining he has her permission (in case any teacher would see him and question him). Unfortunately (for the nurse!) she explained the "zero tolerance" policy. By now I had grown impatient with fellow educators who follow the letter of the law instead of the intention of the law. It upset me that she was more interested in following procedures instead of thinking of a way we could help Chris. So I simply said, "Well, I guess you don't see it as a 'REASONABLE ACCOMMODATION' to allow Chris to carry a pill in his pocket along with a note from you. I suppose you're not concerned he might have a breakdown at school simply because we made it too difficult for him to get the medication he needs." By emphasizing the key phrase, 'reasonable accommodation', she knew I was referring to the ADA and hinting at the rights Chris had under the law she was bound to follow. Fortunately, I was familiar with Chris's rights. I knew in her position she knew about those rights too. It really bothered me that she wasn't cooperative initially, because other parents in my position might not be as familiar with the law regarding disabilities.

My greatest frustration during the ordeal with Chris was when I had to interact with professionals who work with teachers in the field of special education. Having been in special education for 20 years, I was very familiar with their training and responsibilities. It was difficult for me to tolerate psychiatrists, psychologists, special education administrators, teachers, social workers, or nurses who don't do their jobs well. I needed to rely on the Lord for self-control to deal with those professionals who not only didn't support me, but who made my trial more difficult or who spoke harshly with me. During the past year I had encountered excellent and terrible examples in each of the positions listed above. At times even the best, most loving, and capable professionals lacked one critical component in their treatment. There was a need to provide emotional support (e.g., counseling) and resources for the family (especially for the parent who is the primary advocate and caregiver) in addition to Chris. Sometimes I had to ask for feedback, affirmation, guidance, counseling for me. My hope is that someday mental illness will be viewed as alcoholism and terminal illnesses are — as illnesses that affect the whole family. I wrote a letter to Focus on the Family to request a list of Christian resources. They sent me a lengthy list of books, audio-cassette tapes, information sheets, and pamphlets all related to mental illness. They also did what I hope all special educators, health care professionals, and mental health professionals will some day do: they supported me. They had a counselor call to encourage me and to pray with me. It was amazing an organization that large could have a system in place so each letter (from a listener) would result in such a personal response.

My secretary also provided the support I needed so I could help Chris. She frequently asked me how I was doing, and she listened to countless stories of what I had witnessed and heard from Chris. She gave me an audio-cassette tape that had Christian songs of hope and encouragement.

Bill, the guidance counselor, and the nurse at my school were all skilled at ministering to me in addition to caring about Chris. Most of the staff asked me frequently how Chris was doing. Whenever anyone asked me how I was doing, I never really answered that question with more than a brief phrase or a silent expression. I knew everyone who asked really cared and wanted to know, but it was foreign to me to be the one sharing my own personal problems (rather than listening). Furthermore, there just didn't seem any way to adequately explain what it was like to have a child with a distorted mind and literally uncontrollable emotions. Words simply couldn't express all my emotions. It was hard for me to convey the mystery of how I could have tremendous peace and assurance in the midst of unbelievable sorrow. Saying my life seemed surreal at times would be like showing someone a picture of the Grand Canyon or an ice-cream sundae; it would merely be a two-dimensional representation of a multi-dimensional, complicated experience. But Bill, the guidance counselor, and our nurse each had a way of getting me to open up about how I was doing. Many of the teachers obviously were used by God to provide the support I needed to survive the ordeal. Some did it with a gentle loving touch or a hug, some did it with a specific verse or Bible passage, and others did it by solving their own problems at work (so as not to overburden me).

Another example of what I needed desperately and appreciated so much was the support my friend, Jane gave me. Not only did she call to make sure I was alive while Chris was experiencing his psychotic episode, but she continued to regularly call to ask me how I was for months after Chris first got sick. She suggested I research Post Traumatic Stress Disorder (PTSD), since she thought I was experiencing some of the symptoms.

At the local library I found the book I Can't Get Over It: A Handbook for Trauma Survivors *(Second Edition)* by Aphrodite Matsakis, Ph.D. After reading the book, I learned that according to the Diagnostic and Statistical Manual of Mental Disorders (DSM) - VI, I was experiencing mild PTSD. Dr. Matsakis explains that trauma "refers to situations in which you are rendered powerless and great danger is involved. Trauma in this sense refers to events involving death and injury or the possibility of death and injury. These events must be unusual and out of the ordinary, not events that are part of the normal course of life. They are events that evoke a state of extreme horror, helplessness, and fear, events of such intensity and magnitude that they would overtax any human being's ability to cope... You are in a traumatic situation when you either know or believe you may be injured or killed or others about you may be... Just as the body can be traumatized, so can the psyche. On the psychological and mental levels, trauma refers to the wounding of your emotions, your spirit, your will to live, your beliefs about yourself and the world, your dignity, and your sense of security. The assault on your psyche is so great, your normal ways of thinking and feeling and the usual ways you have handled stress in the past are now inadequate."

Dr. Matsakis also explains clearly that in order to qualify as having PTSD, you must not only have experienced true trauma, but you must also meet five additional criteria. The six criteria are thoroughly outlined in her book. The book was helpful to me because I realized much of my behavior was a result of PTSD - a disorder I could do something about. I was experiencing insomnia, irritability, flashbacks and depression around the anniversary of Chris's breakdown, overprotectiveness towards others (Chris, Robert, students at school who were struggling with mental illness), increased physical alertness/hyperalertness at times, and difficulty concentrating at other times.

One reason I decided to write this book was because Dr. Matsakis suggested that writing (journalizing) would be helpful in bringing about healing. Another reason I decided to write this book was because one day I realized Howie had no idea what I had been through with Chris during the two months I was home with him. One day Howie mentioned he had purchased tickets for us to see the musical "Jesus Christ Superstar" because one of the boys' fellow band members was an actor in the musical. Soon after that day we were all in the car and Howie began talking about the musical and started singing some of the songs. When we got home I asked him why he kept mentioning "Jesus Christ Superstar." He looked at me with a blank look that told me he had no idea why I was asking. I asked him if he knew Chris had played that CD nonstop for days when he was "out of it." That's when I realized most of the bizarre and dangerous behaviors occurred during the day when Howie wasn't home. He had no clue what I had gone through. He had some idea, but he certainly didn't know just how terrible it was. When Howie was home in the evening during those two months I was home with Chris, he spent his time with Robert (unless Chris was acting fine, and then he spent time with Chris). So I knew writing this story would help me, let Howie know what it was like (so he could be sensitive to my reactions and behaviors), and minister to others experiencing a similar trial.

Back to Chris's "mini-crisis" in October of his senior year: Once I had successfully arranged to have Chris carry his extra pill in his pocket, the next hurdle was waiting to see if Chris would remember to take it (if he needed it) and then to see if it would work. That was a time when I requested prayers from everyone at school. Even though I had a peace the first day Chris was going to take his extra pill, it was hard for me to concentrate at work. I had to find things to do that didn't require too much concentration, but that involved just enough focus to keep my mind off Chris.

When I picked Chris and Robert up from school, Robert got into the car before Chris. I had a chance to ask Robert how Chris seemed to act. I had gotten into the habit of asking Robert to give me his assessment of how Chris was acting at school. I never realized Robert had grown sick of it, but hadn't told me (all during the spring of Chris's junior year and then during the fall of Chris's senior year). Finally he blurted out he wanted me to stop asking him. I felt so badly that I had made the situation worse for Robert without knowing it. That was the last time I asked him that question.

I found out from Chris and from the band director that Chris was better. When Chris got in the car he wasn't talking nonstop and he didn't sleep on the way home. It seemed like the problem was solved and the crisis was over. But we were heading into another critical period the next month.

November was the month auditions were held for County Band (the best musicians in the county) and District Band (the best musicians in the area - several counties). It was about three weeks after County Band tryouts and the day after the auditions for District Band that Chris suffered his breakdown the year before. I knew it was tremendous pressure for anyone to try out for those bands. The competition is stiff and the stress is high. Whenever I asked for prayer for those auditions, many people asked me if it was wise to let Chris go to the auditions (especially just a few weeks after he had his mini-crisis). But many people couldn't understand what it would have done to Chris if I didn't allow him to try out. He would have assumed I thought he couldn't make it; he would have felt more like a failure; he would have resented his mother controlling his life with things that meant the most to him; and he would have missed out on the opportunity to demonstrate the incredible musician that he is. How could I refuse him the opportunity? And, yet, how could I stand by and watch the added stress harm him?

I came up with a plan to support him as much as possible through the auditions. I made arrangements for Chris to see his psychologist immediately after the County Band auditions. Then when it came time for Chris to travel to another school for the tryouts, I met him there. I was able to honestly tell the hosting school personnel I had to be there because he had a doctor's appointment immediately following his testing.

Robert, who was also auditioning (on the same instrument), had to deal with his mother being at the school. Chris didn't seem to mind. In fact, he seemed like he wanted my support. That concerned me and pleased me at the same time.

I knew Chris would be seeing most of the same students who had auditioned the year before and who had observed Chris demonstrating bizarre behaviors. So, I prepared Chris for what to say and how to act if someone made a reference to his behavior the year before. But I hadn't prepared myself for what I would have to face. How could I have predicted I would witness a thoughtless student from another school imitating what Chris had done the year before (right in front of Chris, Robert, other students, and me!)

When Chris went to District Band tryouts, I met him there too. That time all the students were waiting in the auditorium warming up their instruments. The sound of all the unrelated notes eerily resembled the "music" of a shattered mind. As I walked into the room filled with the blaring, distorted tune, I thought I wouldn't be able to stand staying in there myself. I couldn't imagine how it must have been for Chris who was apprehensive, and maybe a bit distorted himself. I frantically searched the room for Chris with a sense of urgency to get him out of the noise. Usually it was easy to find him because the slide on his trombone was easy to locate among other instruments. The longer it took for me to find him, the more I began to panic, wondering what happened to him. Finally, I spotted him sitting on the stage with his head hung down and his shoulders bent over. He was one of the few students who weren't warming up. He didn't look good to me at all. I was thankful I was there. I waded through all the instruments and students and finally reached him. I asked him if he was allowed to go walk around. Fortunately, he was permitted to leave the auditorium. It was such a relief to retreat to a quiet, peaceful hallway. The Lord even led me to find a way to get him in to do his audition earlier than he was scheduled. While Chris was in a room being tested, two students walked by with trombones and they were commenting about the weird kid who played the trombone who had acted really strange the year before. What were the chances they would be making that comment about Chris at the exact moment they passed me? Once again, my heart was pierced.

Whenever the boys try out for something, I take them out to celebrate even before we find out the outcome. I've tried to teach them it's more important to try your best and then it doesn't matter whether you win or lose. So, I took Chris out to celebrate at a restaurant after the tryouts. Soon after we got the results: Robert and Chris had made County Band, and Chris had made District Band. For any student who is a musician and who achieves such an accomplishment, there is much rejoicing. In Chris's case this was a tremendous testimony of God's provision and Chris's determination, courage and talent. I was grateful God had allowed Chris to see that his life could go on; that his life had been shattered, but miraculously and quickly restored (in one short year).

Chapter 15
Aftershocks and Another Episode

December was a tough month for me because there were so many reminders of the year before. Often something would trigger a memory and I'd experience a flashback. My mind and emotions would instantly be rocketed back to the Christmas season of 1996.

For example, I was at a faculty meeting at school to discuss the elementary Christmas program. The music teacher mentioned one particular grade would sing "Joy to the World." Then she began playing that song. Instantly, I remembered how Chris had played that song repeatedly with his trumpet in a distorted way. I could hear him saying when he sounded his trumpet by playing that song the right way the world would end. I was overcome with emotion. In 1996, when I was helping Chris to return to reality, there was no time to reflect on what was happening. But in 1997, when I unexpectedly was reminded of a particular incident, I had the time to think about what happened. As my mind replayed each awful scene, depression set in. I hadn't had a chance to process my thoughts or work through my emotions. So they caught me by surprise and spilled out at unexpected times.

I was exhausted all the time, so I ate foods with carbohydrates so I would have the energy I needed. But that caused me to gain weight. Knowing how important it was for me to keep my weight down, I went to the doctor to ask him what I could do to deal with my fatigue. He asked if it was possible if I was depressed (and he had no idea about what we had gone through with Chris!). When I responded by saying it was possible, he prescribed Prozac for me to take. Reluctantly, I took the medication. I knew my depression stemmed from the aftershocks of our ordeal. But I also knew I had been depressed when I was in high school, and my own father suffered from depression. I certainly had learned to take mental illness seriously. And I also knew I needed to be strong for Chris. So I took the medication.

Once the holiday season passed, I began feeling much better. So I stopped taking the Prozac. We had a few more months before the next critical period. During the winter months when things were uneventful with Chris, work was busy for me. In addition to my usual responsibilities as Director of Instruction and Director of Special Education, I was planning to have a Math Olympics night and a Bible Olympics during a school day. Applications for new students began pouring in again. With not enough time to do everything at work, I read the new applications at home. So, I was back to spending time working at home. But this time I was careful to spend a more reasonable amount of time on it.

Around that time I got news about a woman I had known from Mercy Christian School. Her husband had died. The memorial service was held in the church affiliated with the school. When I attended the memorial service, I saw many of the teachers I had worked with years before. It was really nice to see them.

I walked through the school building on my way out. I wasn't prepared for the rush of emotions that hit me as soon as I entered the school hallway. Instantly, I had to fight back tears. I didn't even know why I was so upset. I quickly made it to my car. Once in my car I began to sob. I cried because of all the sad memories those corridors held for Chris. I cried because even though there were many sad memories there for Chris, so much more pain had come into our lives since then. I thought to myself life seemed so much simpler then compared to now. That was before my job got so much harder. That was before my father died. That was before we moved several times and before I changed jobs several times. And that was before Chris's breakdown. I also cried because I missed the teachers I had grown to love from there — especially the ones who had been so loving toward Chris. I cried because I missed the days of teaching my own class. I didn't have as many responsibilities, my days were more predictable, and I could nurture one group of students for an entire year. My tears turned to joy, however, as I realized how much the Lord had done in our lives since then. It's strange how the smells of a school building can flood your head with so many memories, emotions, and thoughts.

It was good I had the chance to have a good cry by myself that night in the car. Someone who has been through any crisis needs to cry; it cleanses the soul. Having been through so many sad times with Chris, I've learned to be able to control when I fall apart (usually). One day after a vacation, I arrived at work to discover one of our third grade student's father had died suddenly during the vacation. So I went to the memorial service that day. I knew I couldn't deal with the thoughts and emotions of that sweet child losing her father at such a young age. So I decided not to think about it until later, when I'd be able to let my sorrow out.

During this time the Lord knew we all needed continued healing. The Lord put several godly men in Chris's and Robert's lives. The youth pastor who had spoken with Robert in the hospital (the night we had to admit Chris) periodically called Robert. Usually he called whenever Robert was feeling low for some reason. It was obvious the youth pastor was clearly in tune with the Lord's leading and timing, because he always called at just the right time. The Christian man who provided homebound instruction in Physics and Pre-Calculus for Chris also showed a particular interest in Chris - even long after the homebound instruction was over. Chris often saw him in church. A man named Paul was another special blessing to Chris. He, himself, had suffered from mental illness. He had been hospitalized, too. Paul was a body builder, so he was extremely muscular. But he had the gentlest spirit, too. Whenever he saw Chris in church he gave Chris a big bear hug and a huge smile. He was the one person that could always make Chris smile (a sincere smile). Chris could see how the Lord had helped Paul recover from and survive his mental illness. I was so thankful the Lord had provided such a godly example and mentor for Chris. Chris readily accepted the advice Paul gave Chris because he realized Paul knew what he was talking about.

During that winter the Lord led several parents my way who had children with some sort of mental illness. I soon discovered in most of the cases the mothers of those children couldn't begin to deal with the situation. For example, we had a neighbor who apparently had symptoms of a head injury. But medical tests revealed no evidence of a head injury. All of a sudden, life seemed uncertain for the family because they didn't know what caused the "head injury", and therefore they didn't know what the future would hold. I confided about Chris to the mother because our situations were similar in a way. Soon after, that mother came to tell me the doctors told her the cause of her daughter's apparent head injury was not medical at all; it was psychosomatic. I urged that mother to seek psychiatric help for her daughter because that's who would know how to best help in that situation. The mother asked me not to tell anyone. The mother continued to believe the problems were really medical each time another symptom emerged. It became apparent to me that the mother wasn't emotionally ready to deal with the mental illness; it was easier to go on hoping the cause of the behaviors was really medical.

I also spoke with another mother who had to take medication because she was experiencing panic attacks due to her son's mental illness. Several other parents asked me for advice on how to get their children with emotional problems to agree to speak to a psychologist. Another father of a teenage son with mental illness that prevented him from going to school said he wasn't happy with the psychiatrist they were going to. So I recommended he simply change psychiatrists. With an exhausted tone in his voice he said, "Yeah, I know, but we just can't seem to find the time or the energy to even begin looking for another psychiatrist." I totally understood.

Still another husband and wife were contemplating putting their seriously depressed son in foster care. I found out about that because another mutual friend told me with a critical tone in her voice. I explained that unless you've experienced it, you couldn't understand what it's like to have a child who is suffering from an illness you can't see or measure, and who rejects your love or attempts to nurture. Because of the nature of the illness, parents who need a break cannot even get out together for months at a time.

Around February it was time for Chris to perform in the District Band. He had to stay over night with a strange family in a different school district because the band had to rehearse for two days prior to the performance. It was a lot of pressure for all the teens involved, and especially for Chris. The music they were practicing included things Chris hadn't been exposed to yet (e. g., several changes in time signature in the same song). When I spoke to Chris on the phone the first night, he sounded very stressed. He told me one of the students from his school hadn't played well that day, so the director put him on probation. If that student didn't play better the next day, he would be sent home! I couldn't believe it! When the students had been accepted into the District Band, everyone assumed it was a final decision. Even Chris's school district added a note of congratulations in the newsletter that is mailed to the community. It just didn't make any sense for the director to essentially dismiss a student who had earned a position in the band. Either the student met the qualifications for being in the band or he didn't. The standard couldn't just suddenly change. But if they didn't practice enough, they could be sent home. I began to worry that Chris wasn't thinking clearly under the pressure. But I soon learned what he was saying was true.

When we went to watch the performance I was eager to see Chris. Usually a mother can tell just by looking at her child how he's doing. When I saw Chris he didn't look good at all. He wasn't smiling and he looked very tense. His posture looked strained. Instead of enjoying each song, I prayed Chris wouldn't hit a wrong note. I couldn't wait for the performance to end. It was torture for me. Then it got worse! The announcer introduced a song about a soldier walking onto a battlefield the dawn after a battle. As he walks, he searches for any survivors. As he continues to find more and more carnage, the music builds until he loses his mind. "Until he loses his mind!" I couldn't believe Chris had to play a song about someone losing his mind. I couldn't believe I had to listen to a song about someone losing his mind. Since music is a means of expressing emotions, audiences get caught up in the emotion of performance. As I listened to the clashing notes, my emotions clashed. Pride clashed with pain. As the volume and discord grew, so did my pain. The song filled my head with painful memories of the audition (when Chris was in the noisy auditorium filled with students tuning their instruments). It reminded me of the music Chris played when he was incoherent. It was all I could do to maintain my composure. I began thinking about anything else I could think about - totally unrelated to where I was. The concert ended and it was time to celebrate. It was over, and Chris was fine. He had accomplished one of his goals. And I could relax (for a while).

In March Chris started acting differently in a new way. The first odd incident was when he made a very alarming comment to me. He told me he found the verse in the Bible about what should happen to a child who hits his parents. For some reason, I was familiar with the verse, "And he who strikes his father or his mother shall surely be put to death." (Exodus 21:15). I asked him what he thought when he read that verse. He answered, "I think I got off easy." Chris still didn't understand that his behavior was so different because of his mental illness. He never had been violent to us or to anyone. In fact, he was such a loving and appreciative son. Often he would thank me simply for making dinner.

This nightmare seemed to keep getting worse emotionally for me. It started (just before his breakdown) when I had to listen to hours of stored up pain (relived for both of us). Then I had to watch my 16-year-old son curled up on the floor sobbing, saying, "Why me? I didn't do anything." After that, I had to endure hearing how twisted his (formerly gifted) mind was. Next, I witnessed his explosive and unpredictable emotions, which prevented him from even accepting my attempts to comfort him. Then, I experienced the torment of seeing him revert back to a child in the hospital needing me to stroke him and pleading with me to take him home. Once he became clear thinking, I had to help him deal with the loss of his dream of becoming a drum major. As he recovered, I watched him struggle just to think. And in the spring of 1998 I had to deal with my son's torment of his (unnecessary) guilt feelings for hitting us. It seemed that more was coming.

Early one week he wouldn't respond to our questions or share in our conversations. He stopped smiling again. Then within that week his behavior deteriorated quickly by the day. Each day he seemed worse. We would observe a new "red flag." When we would insist he respond to us, his responses became more belligerent. He asked me, "Don't you ever shut up?" The next day, it took him even longer to respond. He sometimes asked, "What did you say?" I sensed he was having trouble thinking. It was hard for him to process information. Having worked with students who had significant processing delays in their thinking, I knew how to handle the situation. I simply repeated a question calmly and slower, making the words as simple as I could. Everyone was telling me something was wrong (as if I wouldn't notice!). Robert pointed it out, Chris's teachers called to share their observations, and the band director told me. As it got worse, it progressed to the point that Chris wouldn't even answer at all, no matter how many times we asked him something. He started putting his fingers in his ears when I spoke to him. Many people at work said those behaviors sounded like typical teenage behaviors. But Chris wasn't like that. God gives mothers intuition and insight to know when something is really wrong. In my case I knew what was happening. Chris was heading for another psychotic episode. But this time he was experiencing the opposite kind — the kind the student of mine (from the school for the blind) had. Instead of racing, his mind was slowing down. With that type of breakdown the individual eventually appears to be in a catatonic state.

By Thursday of that week Chris sat motionless with his head down most of the time. I knew I needed to take him to the psychiatrist. I knew he needed to stay home on Friday, but he silently refused when I suggested it (glaring at me). Reluctantly, we let him to go to school. The whole family frequently met Chris's physics teacher and some of the students in his class for breakfast Friday mornings at a local diner. After breakfast Howie would take the boys to school on his way to the train station. I would drive my car to work. That morning the waitress was much slower than usual and the boys wanted to stay and finish breakfast. At the last minute, without thinking, we told Chris to drive himself and Robert to school using my car. I would drive Howie to his train station in Howie's car and then pick Howie up at the end of the day.

That day at school was when we had the Bible Olympics I had planned for months. I put in a call to the psychiatrist. I was deeply concerned about what was happening, but I figured Dr. Newman would just recommend a minor adjustment with Chris's medication like before and the problem would be solved. When I spoke with Dr. Newman and described what was happening, Dr. Newman said we needed to bring Chris in to see him first thing the next morning. The urgency and alarm in his voice scared me. I knew we had given Chris the car. What if Chris would lose it completely while driving home from school? I knew I needed to be with him as soon as possible. The elementary school principal was willing to fill in for me with the Bible Olympics, but she was pregnant and was past her due date. So the plan was I would get the Olympics started and she would finish them as long as she didn't go into labor! Once again, the Lord helped me carry on at work as if nothing was wrong. No one would have been able to guess that my son was about to have another breakdown. But the whole staff knew because I needed their prayers again.

At 2:00 PM I left work and flew to Chris's school. I got there before he left. I followed him home from school. That night there was a gym night where the entire school is divided into two teams (by last names, according to the alphabet). Chris was scheduled to be in two events. One of the events was the familiar game "Simon Says" (much like a band march off). I was afraid if he got eliminated and the opposing team cheered, he would run to attack someone. I knew he was extremely unstable. I watched him pacing all night. He behaved fine during his two events. I sat in awe of his drive and his focus to hold it together under all that pressure (in a gym filled with noisy spectators). I sat on the bleachers for several hours watching and studying Chris, all the while praying and poised to leap off the bleachers in case he .....

Thankfully, the evening ended without incident. The next morning we went to see Dr. Newman. After one hour of observing Chris, and talking with all of us, Dr. Newman determined that Chris's medication, which had successfully treated his psychosis, was no longer working. So we needed to wean him off that medication and phase in another type of psychotropic medication at the same time. Once again, it was a very critical time because no one could predict what would happen. Things were so critical, Dr. Newman told us we must get Chris to the psychologist that day and also get the paperwork started at the hospital in case we had to admit him again.

Around that time I was involved in a little campaign to save the music program in the boys' school district. I found myself the chairperson of a steering committee because I opened my big mouth at a band parent meeting. I told the other parents I was tired of going to meetings where everyone just sat around and complained about how and why the music program was declining. I told them I'd be happy to be involved with any constructive efforts to do something about it. So, for several months I had been working with a small committee to address a few specific goals. Right around the time Chris was not doing well was when all our efforts were culminating into one school board meeting. Just days after Chris almost had another breakdown I was scheduled to do a presentation before the board members. The band parents wanted me to speak to some of the school principals and teachers prior to that presentation since I "spoke their language." While I was literally waiting to see if Chris would lose it again, I had to pull off a public relations coup. While I waited to see if the new medication would work or precipitate a psychotic episode, I was preparing for a board presentation. In the evening I had to spend a lot of time with Chris to observe his behavior, to search for any signs of improvement (or otherwise).

We kept Chris home for two days while we were adjusting the medication. The situation was a bit more critical than several months earlier. He was closer to another breakdown. After those two days, it seemed like the new medication was working, but Chris was sleeping most of the time. The psychiatrist recommended we reduce the new medication slightly and give him all of it at night (instead of some in the morning and some at night). It was risky to try anything like that because we didn't want to do anything to precipitate a breakdown. But we had to try it. Thankfully, it seemed to work.

It was hard to tell at times if the new medication was really working or not. For example, some times he wouldn't answer me. When that would happen I never knew for sure whether he was simply being an obnoxious teenager, if his thoughts were really slowing down, or if he was just tired. One night after dinner I was trying to talk to him. I asked him a question and he didn't answer me. I asked him straight out, "Chris, are you having trouble thinking?" He frowned and shook his head, no. So then I repeated my original question and told him to answer. Then I asked him if he was feeling okay. He did answer and said, "I feel fine." So I repeated the original question a third time. When he didn't answer, I told him if he didn't want to talk, he should at least say, "I don't feel like talking right now." He still didn't respond, and just glared at me. Finally I gave into the temptation of showing my frustration and anger. I told him if he was feeling fine and could think, then he should answer me. Since he wasn't talking to me I was going to leave him, and I wouldn't want to talk to him later. I explained if he did that to other people, that's how he pushed people away from him. I walked out of the room.

I flopped onto my bed feeling frustrated and upset with myself for saying what I did. If he really wasn't feeling well, I certainly hadn't made it easy for him to open up to me. But Chris came into my room and sat down, asking me, "Can we talk?" I felt like saying, "Forget it! It's too late now!" I thought he was just playing some kind of annoying game. Then I realized it was possible he really was upset. So I asked him what he wanted to talk about. He told me it was a lot of responsibility to be a squad leader. He was supposed to call all his squad members and remind them to go to an after school practice the next day. I asked him if he was able to remind all his squad members. He said that he had. When I asked him what he was worried about then, he just shrugged. I guessed he was worried about getting reprimanded by the band director if any of his squad members didn't show up. I explained to him that just because his director might try to hold him totally responsible for them getting to practice, he was not totally responsible for their behavior. I explained briefly that in the world many people in business and even education are following Steven Covey's advice in his book <u>Seven Habits of Highly Effective People</u>. In that book Covey talks about two circles: one representing the things we can control (the circle of influence) and the other representing the things we cannot control (the circle of concern). He advocates we should strive to live mainly in the circle of things we can control. I related it to Chris's situation by explaining that Chris could control his own actions. As long as Chris had done what he was supposed to do (call his squad members), then he had been responsible and a good squad leader. If his squad members didn't show up at practice, that would not mean he wasn't a good squad leader; those behaviors were out of his control. I finished that brief conversation by adding that Covey missed the third circle. Christians have three circles in their lives: the things we can control (our free will), the things we cannot control, and the things God controls. I told Chris I strive to have the circle of things I can control remain inside the circle of things God controls.

Chapter 16
Heading to the Finish Line

During Easter vacation Chris seemed happy and relaxed. He was talkative and very much like the Chris that we knew. He even volunteered to tell me his stress level was only "2." Both boys did a little performance for the family. They had memorized the skit, "Who's On First?" by Abbott and Costello. It was wonderful to see them so happy and carefree, with both their minds working so well. So, I felt confident Chris's new medication was working.

But then the night before we all had to return to school, Chris was wandering the house aimlessly. I was trying to refocus and get back into the swing of things. I was trying to remember things like giving the boys lunch money, finding out when I needed to pick them up after school, checking what dinner would be the next day (to see if I had to turn the crock pot on in the morning), looking at what my schedule was for school the next day, etc. Chris kept showing up right near me whenever I turned around.

Finally, I asked him, "Chris, are you just bored, or are you nervous about getting back to school tomorrow?" Since I wasn't very compassionate Chris just glared at me and walked away. I thought, "Perfect! I've just added more stress to Chris and made it difficult for him to talk to me honestly."

Surprisingly, Chris returned to say he was having a difficult time just thinking about going back to school. I suggested we watch a movie to keep our minds off it. I told him he might even be able to fall asleep watching the movie. He liked the idea. Then he asked me another question that made me a bit concerned. He asked if he could sleep in our bedroom. Certainly there was no problem with that. I was happy to do anything to help him relax. It just seemed like an indication of how stressed he was.

For three nights in a row he asked to sleep in our room with us. He even asked me to call Dr. Newman to find out if he could take a tiny bit of his new medication at school when he's feeling extra stress (like he did with the old medication). Since the Spring Arts Festival was approaching, there were many rehearsals at school.

One night Chris made a comment that made no sense to me. He came into our bedroom and Zelda was lying on our bed. Chris patted his thigh to call Zelda to him. Zelda wagged her tail, but remained in our bed. I told Chris to do it again. He said, "She won't come because you yell at her." That comment didn't seem to fully relate to what I had said. I wondered if he wasn't clear in his thinking, or if I simply didn't understand what he meant by that. It was hard not to make a big deal out of every little thing. And yet, I knew that the thing that had helped Chris several times before was catching the "red flags" early.

Chris sometimes still didn't want to hear me talk. I figured since the new medication seemed to be working, he just was tired of hearing from his mother (especially since he was getting closer to graduating and going away to college). But it seemed like he couldn't get away from my words. A local Christian radio had taken a portion of something I had said at an earlier broadcast and incorporated my words into an advertisement for Christian education. Knowing that, I had to remember not to put that station on when I was in the car with him in case he'd hear me! Also, after I did the presentation at the school board meeting, there was an article in the local newspaper with numerous quotes from me. The article was on the front page and so everyone in the band was talking about it. It seemed like Chris couldn't get away from my words no matter how much he (and I) tried!

In the spring we visited the college Chris had chosen to attend. For all college freshman there are many adjustments. Attending orientation days help ease that adjustment. For someone who has recovered from mental illness, more things need to be done to prevent stress and to prepare for the new pressures of college. Selecting a fairly small college campus close to home is wise. Getting involved with fellow Christians (through Christian organizations on campus) would provide support. Sharing helpful and confidential information with the nurse would also be important. Those were the things that preoccupied my thoughts as we spent a day at the college Chris would attend.

It was reassuring to see how happy Chris seemed during his visit that day. I marveled at Chris's courage. Although it would be an adjustment to be on his own living away from home, it was Chris's choice. He was always a risk taker and he was always very focused on achieving his goals.

Easter morning Chris and Robert had to go on a Road Rally to get their Easter treat. Since Chris could drive, I came up with seven tasks for them to accomplish while driving. They both enjoyed it. During the nicer weather the boys began playing tennis sometimes. Robert joined the school's tennis team, but Chris didn't. But Chris was still able to beat Robert at tennis. Chris also joined the church's bowling team. His interest in extracurricular activities suggested that he was feeling well, but he still didn't smile much. I knew that it would be another year or so before he would be "out of the woods."

At 17 years old Chris still asked questions that I don't typically hear from others his age. For example, he asked me, "What can bowling teach us about life?" Having grown accustomed to those sorts of questions, I've learned that Chris really expects a most profound, philosophic answer. I've learned to use those questions as opportunities to share a spiritual truth. Since he asks me those kinds of questions during every day activities, I'm never prepared to ponder a spiritual response. But the Lord usually provides a perfect answer that seems to satisfy him. In that case I told him, "Paul tells us in the Bible that we should be like athletes and keep our eye on the goal. In life we should always have goals. But we need to keep our focus on the smaller steps that lead to accomplishing the larger goals." Chris smiled and nodded in acknowledgment that my answer satisfied him. With Chris older, I didn't have to explain the analogy; he understood it (that in order to made a strike in bowling far down the alley, he needs to focus on the marks much closer to him in the alley).

As it got closer to May, Chris could see the finish line; graduation seemed so close. Just like any typical teen, Chris had senior-itis. It was increasingly harder for him to continue working hard on his schoolwork when he knew he had pretty solid grades - in most subjects. Although Chris was so close to graduating and moving out, my job as his advocate and support wasn't over. He still faced some social and emotional issues, and he was at risk of not graduating.

Even though Chris was generally pretty bright, English wasn't his thing. In fact, he was just average in that area. But in his school district an accelerated English course was the only opportunity for high school students who had been involved in the enrichment program. By his senior year Chris had moved onto the highest level, the Advanced Placement course (which was a college level course). Chris received a 'D' in the first three marking periods in English. The remainder of his grade would be comprised of the last marking period and the two exams (the midterm and the final exam). If he failed the last marking period and either of the major exams, it was possible for him to fail English for the year. I wasn't sure what impact that would have on graduation for him and on his college acceptance.

As the time approached for final exams, Chris informed me he was assigned a project to do in English that would be counted as his final exam grade. He really needed to get a good grade on it. He had other assignments to work on and other exams for which to study. I didn't want to hassle him about his English project because I didn't want to create any undue pressure on him. In spite of my causal reminders, Chris procrastinated to the last minute to work on his project.

When he was down to one last night, he asked me to help him. I reviewed the assignment that indicated the project was a culmination of the entire year. The students were to demonstrate what they had learned about English literature from their four huge textbooks. When I asked Chris to summarize what he had learned, he couldn't begin to tell me anything!!

I immediately went to prayer. We were faced with an impossible situation, and a potentially explosive one. I wanted to kill him. I wanted to yell at him and rebuke him for waiting until the last minute. I would have reminded him he could have gotten help from his teacher before or after school (since his teacher understood Chris's situation and was more than willing to provide extra tutoring).

All of that would have been wasted energy and possibly harmful for Chris. I had no clue where to begin to help him, but somehow the Lord showed me how to guide him. I began with the contents of each book and asked leading questions. That seemed to prompt him to remember what he had learned. Amazingly Chris received a 'B' for that project.

Another situation that was potentially stressful for Chris was the senior prom. Since social issues were the most stressful for Chris he had decided not to go to the prom. When we were talking about it months before the prom Chris smiled and said he would actually rather enjoy riding around in a limousine all night instead!

A few weeks before the prom, Robert asked if he could go to the senior prom with a girl who had suddenly broken up with her boyfriend. She had already bought the tickets, gotten her dress, and arranged for a limousine. Even though Robert was only a sophomore, I thought it was harmless because he would be doing her a favor and they weren't really involved.

The school permitted students who would be attending the prom to leave school early the day of the prom to get ready as long as they had a signed permission slip from a parent. The fact that Robert was going to attend Chris's senior prom really hit home one day. Robert presented the permission slip to me at the same time Chris gave me one to sign. I promptly signed Chris's first without asking any questions. With a surprised look on his face Robert asked, "Why are you signing that for Chris? He isn't even going to the prom." I was certain that Robert wasn't intending to say something that would hurt Chris. He probably viewed my permission as a little deceptive and slightly wrong. I explained to Robert Chris shouldn't be prevented from one of the benefits of being a senior simply because he chose not to go to the prom. I added that he shouldn't have to stay at school when most of the other seniors would be gone. I couldn't resist teasing him by asking why he needed to leave school early - just how much preparation did he need?

When the day came for the prom, Robert was all dressed in his tuxedo looking handsome. Chris waited along with Howie and me for Robert's ride. Howie commented to Robert that he would be the first one in our family who had been in limousine. Howie's comment reminded me that Chris had wished to simply ride around in a limousine instead of going to his prom. I knew when Chris made that comment he was mostly kidding, but I knew part of him would really enjoy the experience. At that moment I decided to surprise Chris with a ride in a limousine after his graduation.

With only a few days left of school I could tell that Chris was cherishing every day that he had with us. He knew that four days after he graduated he would leave to go to Germany for a month. Then he would be home for only several weeks during the summer before he'd have to leave for college.

Those early days in June 1998 were extremely busy for me. I was very busy at school. I had to fill in and teach a second grade class for the last two weeks of school. I was still responsible to handle everything related to my position as Director of Instruction. So I had to do a lot of paper work at home in the evening. At the same time I was planning all the details for Chris's graduation (gifts, party invitations, decorations, the limousine, etc.). We also had to make preparations for Chris's trip to Germany. That involved numerous little details: getting gifts for his host family, doing laundry, getting traveler's checks, going to a meeting at the high school to discuss the itinerary and last minute arrangements, etc. We also were getting Robert ready to go to Vermont with a friend of his for two weeks (during the time that Chris was in Germany). In addition, Robert had to have a mole removed because it looked suspicious to the doctor. All my attention had to be focused on all the details of life and on how Chris was doing. In the business of life I wasn't really focused on my emotions, which was probably good.

Each year in the boys' school district the band plays at graduation. Robert would be playing in the band for Chris's graduation. One night I was upstairs in the bedroom doing some schoolwork and I heard someone playing "Pomp and Circumstance" on the piano (It could have been either one of the boys or Howie). I was immediately overcome with emotion. I found myself sobbing.

School had been such a struggle for Chris. Whenever he had to face difficult social situations, or put up with an insensitive teacher, or handle the challenge of learning organizational skills (which were harder for him to develop) we always promised him things would get easier and some day he would graduate. We assured him that adults aren't as mean to each other as children can be to each other.

The end had arrived so quickly that I was unprepared for the emotion that I would feel. The tears that poured out were for all the pain that he had endured (that we both had endured together), and for the tremendous joy that it was over and Chris had made it.

Only a year and a half before I didn't even know if we'd ever even communicate with my son again normally. I had witnessed a broken mind and a shattered life. But now he was graduating with plans to go to Germany and then to college. What triumph over adversity! What a testimony of God's grace and power! Chris had received the John Philip Sousa band award given "In recognition of outstanding achievement and interest in instrumental music, for singular merit in loyalty and cooperation, and for displaying those high qualities of conduct that school instrumental music requires." Only one student in the school received that award each year.

As I took time to reflect on Chris's life I realized that, like Paul in the Bible, I had "learned to be content in whatever circumstances I am." (Philippians 4:11). Through the worst of it (when I wasn't sure whether Chris would live or die, whether he would ever think rationally again) I was able to trust God to work His plan in my life and believe that He still was a loving God. When I didn't know what the outcome would be I still remained firm in my belief that I serve a loving God who I can trust with my life and my loved ones. I knew that in this life God told us that we would have tribulation. But that through it all God would sustain us and use any situation for His kingdom.

I was familiar with those Bible heroes who suffered greatly and yet were still able to believe in a loving God - the God of the universe and the King of all kings. So I never doubted that their God who is the same yesterday, today, and forever would remain faithful to me no matter what would happen to Chris. I never expected God to protect me from the tragedies that other Christians have to face all the time. So, I knew that it was all by God's grace - everything - that Chris was graduating, that I still had my sanity - everything was because of God's grace.

Chapter 17
Suicidal Thoughts

When summer arrived Chris and Robert were both away for one month. Chris was in Germany and Robert was at a Christian camp. Although school ended for the students, I still went to work because I was part of the office and administrative staff. But we worked fewer hours and took two weeks off for a vacation.

My freedom from responsibilities with the boys and work allowed more time to think. My thoughts naturally turned to the next chapter in my life: Chris leaving home to go to college. When most mothers reach the milestone of their first child leaving home (either to go to college, to get married, or to move out), they are very emotional. For me it represented a huge step in faith. To say that I felt strong emotions would be an understatement. It would be more accurate to say that I was depressed.

At first I was unaware of how depressed I was. I chose to take several weeks off from work right after school ended. Those days passed by silently. During the day I had no need to speak to anyone and was content to stay at home alone. When Howie came home after work I didn't feel like talking to him. With both boys away and with nothing to share about work, there seemed no need to talk to Howie. I felt very sad and chalked it up to missing the boys. But there was a part of me that knew I was experiencing something far more significant than sadness.

My depression became darker and deeper. I had a constant melancholy feeling. All I wanted to do all day was lie around. I knew that this was a reaction to the pain I had experienced during the past year and a half. I didn't have to be strong for Chris because he was in another part of the world. So I fell apart. I just wanted the pain to end. Suicidal thoughts began to cross my mind. Thoughts of the boys, however, prevented those suicidal thoughts from taking hold of my mind.

My pity party grew more elaborate. I wondered who would take care of me. Did Howie even notice that I was depressed? Did he even care? The more days that passed with Howie not addressing my problem the more my anger, pain, and discouragement grew.

It was at a marriage counseling session with a pastor that I was shocked back into my functioning mode. The pastor asked me how long I planned on not speaking to my husband, implying that my silence was sin. My initial thought was, "He doesn't realize that it's all I can do from killing myself! Life is an effort for me. I'm not able to make any effort with anyone, let alone my husband." Then it was clear to me...I needed professional help.

The next day I scheduled an appointment with Chris's psychologist. At the session with him I explained what condition I was in emotionally. With significant concern and urgency, he told me that I had been through a very serious trial with Chris. After hearing my symptoms, he concluded that I was experiencing clinical depression. It was time for me to take care of myself. He instructed me to make an appointment with my physician and tell him that my psychologist recommended medication for my depression.

Since I knew that my pain was a result of what I had been through with Chris, I initially didn't think it was right to take medication. It didn't make sense to take a pill for a bad memory. Depression clouds your thinking. But I had learned to respect mental illness. I knew that clinical depression was not something to take lightly. I knew that just as medication can effectively treat a physical illness, medication can effectively treat a mental illness (which is actually a physical illness also). After a visit with my physician, I began taking Prozac again. It gave me a headache and I gained weight, but I started to feel better.

By the time both boys returned I was able to function again. I was able to go through the motions of preparing Chris to go away to college. I attempted to crowd out emotions about college by cluttering my mind with the details of college. I made lists of what to buy and what to pack.

It was a relief to have both boys home again. Chris returned from Germany with many gifts for the family. Among the gifts to me was a beautiful skirt. It was amazing that Chris was able to select a skirt that not only fit me but one that was a style that I would have selected myself.

Robert returned from camp wearing a beard!!! It was quite an odd feeling to see our youngest son with a beard. No longer could we perceive him as our baby. It was evident that he was a young man. Both boys returned with many stories to share about their vacations.

Since Robert had participated in a counselor training program, he had spent several grueling weeks. He spent one week canoeing approximately 90 miles. Then he hiked back those same miles on the Appalachian Trail. After that he spent a week rock climbing. Although Robert was in a male group, he managed to find females along the Appalachian Trail. Amazingly, he ran into some "cute" teenage girls who were also hiking the same part of the trail.

By the time Chris had to go to college I felt emotionally stronger and up to the task of letting him go. The day we took him to college we had to take two cars to fit all his stuff. Robert happily came along to share his muscles and to see the college again. When we arrived at the college we were directed to the area to unload. There, waiting for each freshman, was an army of upperclassmen (male and female) with open arms prepared to help the new students move in. Robert couldn't believe his eyes. Females waiting to greet us! Howie simply said, "Down boy!" From then on Robert couldn't wait to go to college.

I noticed that the guys moving in to college were not nearly loaded down with belongings as the girls. It didn't take that long for us to help Chris move in. He wanted to unpack his things himself. Before I knew it, it was time to say good-bye. I had successfully managed to deliver my son to college without getting upset. Just as I was hugging Chris good-bye, he said, "Isn't this the time that you share some motherly wisdom with me, Mom?" Of course I hadn't prepared any pearls of wisdom. I had forced myself to do just the opposite. I didn't want to think about the fact that we were turning the page to a new chapter in our lives. All I could think of was to remind him that the Lord is with him everywhere - even at college. Perhaps that was what I was reminding myself.

As we drove home my head was flooded with questions. Would he remember to take his medication? Would anyone find out about his medication and his condition? How would he get along with his roommate? How would he handle any stress that came his way? Would he make friends with anyone? Would he call?

Wondering can easily lead to worrying. So I stopped wondering and focused on the fact that Chris planned on coming home every weekend, at least during marching band season. Anyone can make it only five days apart from a loved one.

But then my mind would wander again. What would the future hold? Would Chris remain strong emotionally and mentally?

Chapter 18
Enough is Enough

The first few weeks of college seemed to be running smoothly. We communicated daily with Chris by computer. But Chris preferred to hear our voices and called frequently. He sounded good. He seemed to be enjoying his classes. He especially enjoyed his schedule, which allowed him to sleep in until noon just about every day. He tolerated my motherly interrogation and reassured me that he was eating at the cafeteria, wearing warm clothes, and getting enough rest. He even answered more sensitive questions such as if he was interacting with others for fun (rather than isolating himself). It was very stressful for him to attempt to make new friends. The fear of rejection was his greatest fear.

Only one month into his first semester at college Chris's roommate said that he wanted another roommate. It wasn't that he didn't like Chris. He was very nice to Chris. He had made a friend who was a fellow athlete. I began to anguish over the thought of Chris experiencing one more social blow. But then I realized that he could have far worse problems with his roommate (one that takes drugs, one that makes excessive noise, one that parties in the room all the time, etc.). Since Chris didn't agree to trade roommates, his original roommate was rarely in the room. He spent most of his time in class, in sports, or with his new friend. A roommate that was rarely there was actually the least stressful situation for Chris.

As planned, Chris came home every weekend to see us and to see his former marching band. Robert was a drummer in the band. It was wonderful to see Chris. He seemed happy. But something wasn't right with him physically. At first we noticed that he was walking sort of stiff-legged, like a robot. He complained of sore heels. Thinking that he had slightly injured his heels from all the years of marching, we bought him some orthodics for his shoes. The plastic insoles were supposed to provide the added support and comfort he needed. But each week we saw him he seemed worse, not better.

After about two months Chris began to complain of a sore back and shoulder. We thought all the books he carried across campus caused it. Each time we saw him, however, he seemed increasingly stiffer. I was afraid his medication was causing a side effect called tardive dyskinesia, which causes rigidity. So I called his psychiatrist. The psychiatrist asked if I had contacted Chris's primary physician. Since I hadn't, he wanted me to begin investigating the cause there and suggested that Chris get some blood tests.

By the time Chris saw his physician the stiffness had spread to his entire body. He couldn't turn his head, rotate his arms, or bend over to put on his shoes. When Dr. Kent saw him, he was shocked at the severity of Chris's condition. He immediately identified it as Rheumatoid Arthritis. Every joint in Chris's body was extremely stiff and sore. Dr. Kent couldn't believe that Chris had been walking around campus for several months with that amount of pain. He couldn't tell us what caused the arthritis. He said that the blood tests might indicate the cause of the arthritis. We had to wait for several days for the results. In the meantime, Chris was put on an anti-inflammatory drug to treat his arthritis.

It was right before Christmas and time for Chris to take his first finals. In the beginning of the week of finals Chris sounded very upset. I asked him if he was concerned about his finals. He answered, "No. I'm upset because they closed the game room in the student center, so I can't play pool. Now I don't know what to do." I suggested that he study for his finals. He said, "I don't know what to study." I told him, "Just study your notes." That's when I found out that he hadn't taken any notes in most of his classes. The only notes he took were some math formulas that he programmed in his graphing calculator. In a shocked tone I responded, "Chris, you HAVE to take notes. How do you think you can pass any tests without taking notes? That's what people do in college; they take notes." Chris calmly reminded me that he had passed all his tests during the semester so far without studying. I was left speechless. I didn't know what to recommend. I couldn't relate to someone who didn't need to study in college. Chris finished his first semester with a 3.0 (B) average.

Several days before Christmas Chris was home for the semester break and we got a call from Dr. Kent. He had the results of the blood tests. With stammering and halted words, he told me that he thought Chris might have lupus. Dr. Kent even said, "No one wants to hear they have lupus, so we'll need to have Chris seen by a specialist - a rheumatologist to confirm it."

When I hung up the phone I went directly to our computer. I didn't know anything about lupus, but Dr. Kent's tone and words hinted that it was something awful. On the Internet I found the National Lupus Foundation that included a chat room. I typed in the details of our situation (Chris's age, symptoms, and initial diagnosis from the doctor). Someone suggested that I buy *The Lupus Book; A Guide for Patients and Their Families by* Daniel J. Wallace, J. D. I immediately called several local bookstores to see if they had the book in stock. No one had the book in stock, so I had to order it. Then I waited for the book to come in. As I waited, I wondered what was so awful about that disease.

The book arrived Christmas Eve. Since I was busy making our Christmas Eve dinner, I didn't have time to begin reading the book. Anxious to know something, I read the inside cover of the book. I learned that lupus is a disease of the immune system. The body becomes allergic to itself. It is a condition where a person's antibodies attack good cells. The book explained that there are two types of lupus: organic and non-organic. The non-organic type is chronic, but not usually fatal. However, the organic type can be fatal. Once the kidneys are attacked the patient can die. Often with the organic type the brain is the first to be attacked and the patient has a psychotic episode. When I read that I realized that if Chris had lupus he had the organic type. Then I read on. "More than 90 percent of all lupus patients in the United States live more than 10 years after being diagnosed. The survival of patients with organ-threatening disease is still an unsatisfactory 60 percent at 15 years." Could it be that Chris had just received a death sentence? Would he face a series of flares, or flare-ups, as different organs were attacked? He had just overcome tremendous odds and was beginning a new and exciting phase of his life. How could I even bear the thought again of losing him? As I sat on my bed reading those words over and over again through tears, Robert came in. I realized that sooner or later he would have to know. I figured that it was better for Robert to know why I was crying rather than offer no explanation. He was old enough to know what was going on with his brother. Surely he had seen enough so far. So on Christmas Eve I had to tell Robert that his brother might have a fatal disease.

The appointment for the rheumatologist was scheduled for February. We had to wait two months because he was such a well-respected doctor in the area. But that meant we had to wait two months to find out whether or not Chris had lupus.

During Christmas break Chris spent a lot of time playing pool. We bought a pool table for the family rather than spending money on a lot of gifts the boys didn't really need or want. Chris had begun to play a lot of billiards and Ping-Pong at the student center at college. In addition, we had Robert's sixteenth birthday party at a billiard hall. Robert's friends loved playing pool and visited often to play. Sometimes I watched Chris and Robert playing pool or playing their trombones together and wondered if there would soon be an end to their happy times together. The thought of losing Chris tormented me and wouldn't escape me.

The day came for Chris to see the rheumatologist. The plan was that Howie would drive Chris into the city for the appointment and I would meet them there (since I couldn't take off from work). As I drove toward the city I realized that in a few short minutes I would find out Chris's fate. I had tried to ignore my fears for two months, but it was getting harder as I got closer to the hospital. It was as if I was going to hear a sentence from a judge (life or death).

When I reached Center City and was only a few blocks from the hospital my anxiety had grown. As I drove slowly through the stop-and-go traffic, I noticed that the narrow city streets were filled with teenagers and young adults. They were obviously not businessmen and businesswomen. I also noticed many police officers. In my anxious condition I imagined the worst: something was "going down." Then I heard what sounded to me like gun shots in rapid fire. Then I began praying, "Lord help me to arrive at the hospital safely. Help me to find a safe place to park." Later that night I found out that the people were celebrating the Chinese New Year. What I had heard were firecrackers. How would I know? My whole life was absorbed in Chris's condition. I had grown to expect the worst as a way of preparing myself for whatever would come my way.

Thankfully we learned that Chris did not have lupus. All my worrying was in vain. The rheumatologist confirmed that he did have rheumatoid arthritis. However, he could not identify the cause. He instructed Chris to continue taking his anti-inflammatory medication for six months. He said that after six months if he discontinued the medication and had no more arthritis pain then the arthritis was caused by a virus that had run its course. If, however, his arthritis pain continued then it means that Chris most likely had early onset of rheumatoid arthritis.

Six months later we found out that Chris still had arthritis pain, which meant that he would be facing a lifetime of arthritis pain, unless medication could effectively treat it. During the six months Chris had tried three different medications. Each medication took all but 25 percent of the pain away. But that remaining pain really discouraged Chris. He was tired of feeling sick and having to face medical problems. When he got a virus his arthritis pain increased making a typically lousy virus even worse.

Around that time a friend mentioned that she heard of a supplement called Mega MSM. People with rheumatoid arthritis were getting complete relief from the supplement. I was reluctant to

145

get the supplement for Chris because his physician didn't know anything about it. We couldn't be sure how it would interact with all his other medications. Since it was unusual to hear Chris complain, I ordered the supplement and gave it to Chris. The results were amazing! He was free of his arthritis pain.

Robert was in his junior year of high school. He was a squad leader in the marching band. He was just as popular as ever, especially with the girls. Since I was still involved with the band parent booster organization, I knew many of his friends' parents quite well. On several occasions I found out information that he didn't know about his female admirers. Robert was eager to hear the news. Knowledge is power. It was good for Robert to know that the parent network was alive and well.

Robert decided to try out for drum major. I prepared myself for the emotional blow that might come when Chris heard the news. When Chris was in high school he hoped to be the drum major of the marching band. Everyone agreed that he was next in line for the honor. But then he got sick. Even after Chris's illness the band director said that Chris would be a "strong contender" for drum major. But he cautioned that the pressures of the leadership position might be too great so soon after Chris's illness. That was a tremendous loss for Chris. He probably would never have another opportunity to become a drum major.

Chris's response to the news was a testimony of his character. He offered to help Robert prepare for the auditions. He gave Robert tips on conducting. He also had Robert practice teaching a marching lesson, giving him feedback afterwards. It was a blessing to see how much Chris loved and supported his brother, and how much Robert respected Chris.

At a follow up visit with his primary physician Chris had to have some blood tests. The results of those blood tests revealed that Chris had a thyroid problem. I couldn't believe that there was something else Chris had to deal with. Fortunately his newly diagnosed condition could be treated with medication. That made it a total of fourteen pills that he took each day.

Chris was in his second semester of his freshman year of college. One evening we received a phone call from him informing us that he lost his backpack. It contained several textbooks, his notes for a paper he started to write, his checkbook, his graphing calculator (with formulas that he had programmed), and other less significant items. Such a loss could be extremely stressful. Many adults who lose their wallet or purse consider it a major inconvenience or even a crisis. Chris couldn't study for an upcoming test because his textbook was gone. He couldn't even buy a replacement book because his checkbook was gone.

It was encouraging to hear how clear-headed Chris was in the midst of his problem. He acted very responsibly, thinking of everything possible to do. He retraced his steps and looked everywhere he had been (several times). He reported the missing backpack to the campus police. He even went to the bookstore to alert them in case his book showed up there.

I felt so badly for Chris. There wasn't much that I could do. I decided to show my support by driving to campus and surprising him. I bought a new graphing calculator, drove to his college, and went directly to the bookstore to buy a replacement book. That's when I found out that Chris found his backpack. He was even considerate enough to let the bookstore know. Chris's response to the whole incident demonstrated how well he could handle a stressful situation on his own. If I were God I wouldn't have put him through that. But having been through it we all realized that Chris was mentally and emotionally stronger.

One evening Howie casually mentioned, "Oh, by the way, Chris is bleeding a little bit from his butt." I responded, "What do you mean? That's not normal! How long has it been going on? How much is he bleeding? Where exactly is the blood coming from?" Howie didn't know exactly. All he could tell me was that there seemed to be a little hole right near his tailbone. That's where the fluid seemed to be seeping.

When we took Chris to the doctor we found out some good news and some bad news. The bad news was that he had a pilonidal cyst. He had a cavity near his tailbone that would have to be corrected surgically. The good news was that it was unrelated to any of his other conditions. The other good news was that he could wait until the semester ended to have his surgery.

As it got closer to the end of the school year we got more anxious to hear if Robert got selected to be drum major. If Robert got selected it would be quite an honor. We prayed for God's will in the decision, but were hoping that he would make it. With tongue in cheek, Robert boiled it down to one little difference. He said, "If I become drum major I'll be marching in the parades backwards. If I don't make it, I'll march forward." The announcement would be made at the band banquet (that was just for the students). After the banquet Robert told us he would be marching backwards in the parades.

During the summer vacation Robert would be attending a one-week training camp for drum majors. In addition, he would be spending a month away at a Christian camp as a counselor-in-training. I was concerned about what Chris would do during the three months he had off for summer break. Without a job he would be the only one home during the day.

Chris applied for a job at Howie's company. They usually needed summer help. The pay was good, the building was air-conditioned, and Chris could ride in and out of the city with Howie on the train. They could also meet and have lunch every day. In addition, even though the job was an entry-level position, it would be good for the company to get to know Chris. Once Chris graduated from college he could apply to that company for a permanent position related to his chosen profession (business).

The only potential problem that threatened Chris's chances of working at Howie's company was Chris's surgery. He was scheduled

148

to have the surgery right after the semester ended in May. He would have to start working only about a week after the surgery. Thankfully, Chris got the job. But that meant that he would have to ride a train for about 45 minutes each way with a sore bottom. As usual, Chris was up for the challenge.

It was fortunate that Howie worked in the same building. If Chris's bandages needed to be changed Howie could change them. Sometimes Chris's blood would saturate his bandages and seep right through his pants. Thankfully, that didn't happen when he was at work. I was so thankful, too, that Howie didn't mind changing Chris's bandages. I didn't mind the butt thing; it was the blood that nauseated me. On a follow-up visit I went with Chris rather than Howie. All that the surgeon was supposed to do was check how the healing was going.

In the treatment room Chris laid down on his stomach. Although he was 18 years old, he still appreciated having his mother standing right by him. As I stroked his head lightly the doctor checked his incision. The doctor was not pleased with how it was healing. It wasn't healing from the inside out, which meant that another cavity might form. He informed Chris that he would have to make a "little incision" so that it would heal correctly.

I was probably more apprehensive than Chris. There was no way I wanted to see the doctor make his little incision. Since I was still standing next to Chris's head, I simply avoided looking at what the doctor was doing. But the doctor kept giving Chris a blow-by-blow description of what he was about to do. "I'm going to numb you now.... Now I'm going to make a little incision..." Then I heard a gurgling sound mixed with the sound of air escaping. I asked, "Is that sound coming from Chris?" The doctor informed me that he had to express the fluid that was in the cavity. As Chris lay there feeling no pain, I began to feel light-headed. The doctor asked, "Are you all right?" Chris answered, "Yea, I'm fine." The doctor responded, "No, I mean is your mom all right?" I welcomed that as my opportunity to sit down (before I fainted or threw up!).

On the way out to the car Chris was feeling really discouraged. He knew that this slight set back would make his recovery longer. He was tired of being sick. The anesthesia was wearing off and his incision was starting to hurt. I felt just as discouraged. We could have both had a real good pity party. I knew I couldn't offer any sincere words of encouragement, so I thought humor was in order. I sarcastically said, "How do you think I feel? I had to hear some pretty disgusting sounds coming from your butt. I don't think that those sounds should come from someone's butt. I almost fainted or threw up!" Chris didn't miss a beat. He responded by doing a pretty good imitation of the sound!! He could redirect his focus from his pain to inflicting pain on his mother. Periodically during the ride home he let me relive the awful experience by providing the sound effects.

Chris wasn't the only one with significant health problems that year. My cousin (and one of my best friends) found out that she had breast cancer. She handled the crisis with style and dignity. As was typical of our family, she kept her sense of humor through it all. But there were times when it was difficult to keep a sense of humor (like the day she decided to shave her head because her hair was coming out in clumps from the chemotherapy). She had beautiful, long, thick, wavy auburn hair. Her husband had first noticed her because of her hair. That's why it was so difficult to see her without her hair. But even without her hair she looked like a model. With a slender and tall body and with perfect taste in clothes she was a fashion statement - even with cancer. Several years earlier she had to have surgery for a pilonidal cyst. So she and Chris could compare notes.

When school ended for Robert in June the pace of life slowed down. Robert was getting ready to go away to camp. Chris had just started his job at Howie's company. Finally I could relax and recover from the emotional year of medical treatments for Chris and for my cousin. But God had something else in mind.

One week after school ended for the students at my school I came down with viral meningitis. People asked me how I got it. After researching it a bit, I learned that you can either get it from a mosquito bite, or from someone carrying the virus. I learned that about 20 percent of the adult population carry the virus at one time or another, but don't contract the disease because their immunities fight it. My pace at work must have weakened my immune system. For seven weeks straight I had been pushing myself beyond my limit. In addition to all my regular responsibilities as Director of Instruction, I organized the achievement testing for the elementary school, I organized the math and Bible Olympics, and I substituted for about a month for a second grade teacher in our school. While I was substituting I not only had to grade papers, plan lessons, and write tests, but I also had to do all my other work (which I did before, during, and after school). I was working every waking minute late into the nights for seven weeks. I learned the hard way that my body is not a machine.

I was too sick to say, "Enough is enough!" The excruciating pain in my head lasted about five days. During those five days I couldn't move my head at all without severe pain. I couldn't open my eyes or even talk because the input would cause pain. My eardrum was perforated and both ears were clogged. The severe pain caused me to vomit. The doctor wanted to hospitalize me, but I preferred to stay home. He said that if I got dehydrated or couldn't manage the pain I would have to be hospitalized. Finally, the most severe pain subsided.

That U-turn in life is what God used to alter my life for the following year. Instead of working full time, I became the consultant for the school. In addition, I worked on some curriculum for another Christian organization. That allowed me the time to rest and recover. It also permitted me the time to spend with Robert during his last year at home (before going away to college). The meningitis was a blessing in disguise.

151

Chapter 19
"A Few Weak Limbs"

When I shared my completed manuscript with a close friend of mine, she informed me that it wasn't finished. At the time this chapter wasn't written. She knew that there was an entire segment of my journey that I hadn't written about. In order to protect my husband I hadn't written about the difficulties we had in our marriage. My friend and I knew that having a child with special needs puts more pressure on a marriage. More time, effort, and attention need to be devoted to the child. There are many more problems to solve (than in a family with children who don't have any special needs). Therefore, the husband and wife need to be able to effectively solve problems, work through conflict, communicate, and support one another. The problem is that all marriages involve two people who bring to the relationship issues from their past. It's a formula for disaster when you add additional pressures. Therefore marriages that involve a child with special needs are at greater risk of divorce.

So if I knew this issue was an important part of the picture of my life, why didn't I include it throughout my story so far? It's because I was raised to keep those things private. We all cope with life in our own ways. In my mother's effort to protect my father she kept his breakdown and depression a secret from most people for years - even from my brother, my sister, and me. We never discussed the details of his tragic and abusive childhood. All I knew were the major incidents: my father's identical twin died as a child when a rat bit him, his biological father was killed in a war, his mother remarried simply to help her cope with all her children (I was never quite sure how many), his step-father had his arm blown off in a war and was left disabled, and my father left home as a child to escape abuse and worked on a farm to earn his room and board. I also knew that my father's older brother helped pay for my father's college. And I knew that my father earned his master's degree and successfully earned a living for us the whole time he was alive.

As I grew up I began to learn other things. It wasn't until I was diagnosed as having Impaired Glucose Tolerance that I found out that my mother probably had the same condition her whole life. So I was taught to keep things private. But as I grew up and learned more about God's ways I learned that we are commanded to comfort one another with the comfort we receive from God. The Lord wants us to encourage others with the hope that we have in Him.

The friend that encouraged me to add this chapter had also experienced many of the difficulties that I've had to deal with. We would compare notes without having a pity party. She and I were similar in that we were both strong and constructive. In telling me what I had left out of the book she reminded me that we both had "a few weak limbs" in our marriage. I just loved the analogy, but thought it was a huge understatement. I responded, "'A few weak limbs?!' The whole trunk is rotting!!" We laughed, but behind the laughter was a somber truth: the whole trunk was rotting.

To understand the issues I should begin with a relationship I had before I met Howie. In high school I dated mainly one guy. Even his parents warned me not to get involved with him. My parents had their concerns as they saw me getting more involved with him. I even decided not to go to college so that I could marry him right after high school. That shocked my parents because I had been on an accelerated track in high school. College was always in the plans for my future. My parents got me to agree to a compromise; they said I only had to go away to college for one year. Early in the fall of my first year of college I began to hear news about my fiancée that was very upsetting and difficult for me to comprehend. First I found out that his parents kicked him out of their house because he embezzled money from them. Then I found out that he had moved in with a close friend and embezzled money from his friend's parents. So his friend kicked him out of his house. Then my parents let him move in with them. Once again he embezzled money from them. This time he left their home and disappeared. The police were looking for him.

154

It seemed like each week I discovered another awful fact about him. I couldn't believe all that was happening. My roommate at college tried to console me. After a month of my continued ritual of hearing bad news and then having a sobbing fit, my roommate got frustrated. She had grown weary of comforting me only to see me upset the next day. In her frustration, she told me that she didn't believe that I was really a Christian - that if I was really a Christian I would trust that the Lord would help me no matter what happened. Having said that she walked out abruptly and left me alone. It was the spiritual slap in the face I needed. She was right. I had been raised in a religious family. We faithfully went to church every Sunday and said grace every night before dinner. My mother and father were very involved in serving in various capacities at church. So I grew up thinking I was a Christian without ever really having a relationship with the Lord.

I sat there pondering whether everything I had learned in church was a lie or pretend, or if it was true. I wondered if there really was a God who loved me, and if Jesus really died on the cross for me. I was faced with a decision to believe or not. I decided that it was all true. As soon as I made that decision I immediately felt an unusual peace flowing throughout my entire being. Even though I didn't know what would become of my life (considering the situation with my fiancé), I had an assurance that I would be Okay, because I believed that there really was a God that cared about me. Shortly after that I went to a women's Christian gathering with my mother were I made a public acceptance of Jesus as my personal Savior and Lord.

The situation hadn't ended yet with my fiancé. I hadn't seen him since I started hearing all the shocking news. Finally he showed up and I went home for the weekend. Many people who were involved in the situation met at my parents' house to confront him. It was then that I learned that his entire life had been a lie. He had totally fabricated a bank account. He even showed me a bankbook, which I later learned wasn't real. He told everyone that he had a job, but he didn't. He would leave his house in the morning supposedly to go to work, hide in the bushes, and then go back to his house when everyone else had gone.

I couldn't believe that I had been deceived so badly. I felt so dumb, so naive, and so ashamed. I also felt responsible for what I had put my parents through. But yet I felt thankful that the experience is what led me to a saving knowledge of the Lord. Now I had something real to hold onto.

In the spring of 1973 I first met Howie at college. He and I were seeing other people. We were just friends. I didn't want to get involved with anyone. But gradually we became closer and got more involved, and we stopped seeing other people. Our relationship developed into something that was very intimate and physical. Howie had been raised Catholic, and I was a new Christian so neither of us were convicted about our lifestyle together. Even after Howie accepted the Lord as his Savior we continued with our intimate relationship. We had an understanding.

I graduated college one year before him and got a job in another state. That's when the problems began. While Howie was at college without me he was with another woman. We talked on the phone regularly, wrote notes to each other often, and saw each other almost every weekend. Howie never told me what he had done. I learned about it by accident. I was devastated. Not only was I hurt by the betrayal, but also it opened the recent wound of having been deceived by my former fiancé. I broke up with Howie.

I was alone and had just started my first professional job. It was a real test of my faith. New teaching friends of mine tried to help me by encouraging me to go out with them. That didn't help. I had fallen in love with Howie and believed that we would some day get married. But then all that seemed to be over. I was so confused. One night when I was walking my dog I looked at all the Christmas decorations that were up and I felt so alone. I felt so broken hearted, but I suddenly realized that God must have something in store for me that would be even more wonderful than marrying Howie. With renewed hope I felt at peace with my situation.

When I returned to my apartment I received a phone call from Howie. He told me that he wanted to ask me to marry him during Christmas vacation, and that he wanted me to pray about it before then. I was more confused than ever!! I had just resolved that I would be Okay if I didn't have Howie in my life. Actually, it would have been easier to end the relationship. I couldn't stand to be hurt again, and definitely not by Howie. That would have been too painful. I really didn't want to trust him again. I wasn't ready to become vulnerable. But I wanted to do what the Lord wanted, so I prayed about my decision. I didn't know the answer until Howie began to propose. Then I immediately knew that it was yes. My life was back on track. We started making the wedding plans.

Then the unthinkable happened shortly after that. I had a roommate in my apartment. One weekend Howie came to visit and we had a really big snowstorm. My roommate's college was closed and Howie couldn't leave. In spite of all the snow I had to get to work. Since I worked at a residential school for the blind the teaching staff had to make every effort to get to work to relieve the child care workers. When I returned home from work Howie was in the shower and my roommate wasn't there. Then I received a phone call from my roommate who was crying and telling me that Howie had made some advances. I was devastated and confused.

Since I had prayed about my decision to marry Howie, I believed that it was God's will for us to marry. But given the circumstances I wasn't sure of anything. The one thing I did know was that I still wanted to seek God's will for my life. I asked my mother to pray about whether I should go ahead with the marriage, since I knew that I was too upset to be able to discern His will for me.

After several days my mother informed me that she believed that it was the Lord's will for Howie and me to get married. So right from the start our marriage was a step in faith for me.

In the early years of our marriage I believe God honored my obedience to His will and helped me to trust Howie again. But there were other issues that were surfacing. Howie 'let' me do all the disciplining of the boys. He used to boast proudly about what a good job I did with them. Chris was difficult to manage, but I was able to handle him and act as an advocate for him.

However, I grew tired of handling Chris's needs all alone. In the early years of our marriage I didn't resent Howie for not being involved because I rationalized that it was my job since behavior management was a strength of mine. When Howie was working on his master's degree I would take the boys out of the house so that he could study. It was very difficult for me to think of places to take an extremely hyperactive son but I was happy to do all I could to help Howie.

It was also up to me to do all the housework and the meals. Before I went back to teaching (when Robert was four years old) it was possible for me to do it all. But when I started working outside the home I was exhausted from teaching, cooking, cleaning, taking the boys to their activities, handling Chris's behavior problems and helping him with his homework, and all the rest. There wasn't much energy left for me to devote to Howie.

After Howie got his master's degree I started working on my master's degree. When I was in my last semester Chris was in fifth grade. I was teaching second grade, applying to about 30 public school districts, getting the house packed up and ready for us to move, and dealing with the fact that my father was dying of cancer. In addition to all that, things were really bad for Chris at school. I had to deal with him getting beat up, unfairly punished at times, having him run away from school, etc. It was then that I found out that Howie had been unfaithful to me. But once again I found out about it only after Howie had tried to keep it from me.

Howie found a lump on his abdomen. He told me about it and said he would have it checked out by the doctor. When Howie got the results he proceeded to share them with me. He looked more serious and scared than I had ever seen him. I thought he was going to tell me he had cancer. Instead he told me that he had contracted some sexually transmitted disease.

With those words my life stopped. There are no words to describe how a woman feels at a time like that. I wasn't hungry. I didn't want to do anything at all. Being in education I often witness the pain divorce brings to the children. I wondered how a mother could allow difficulties in a marriage to affect her own children. Then I realized that the union between a husband and a wife is stronger than maternal love. When a man and woman marry the two become one. I believe that God knits their souls together when they make their vows before God. So when one partner has committed adultery there is a ripping of that bond - a violation to the deepest dwelling places of one's soul. For me the pain was worse than when my own father died. Nothing mattered to me any more. Since Howie had unprotected sex I also considered the possibility that we could both contract HIV and eventually die from AIDS.

I was determined not to allow the boys to be victims. I hoped that there was still a chance to end the tragedy with me before all our lives were shattered. I knew that there was no way any female could ever hide such hurt. I knew that most women couldn't ever forgive such betrayal. But I knew that God is able to do beyond all that we imagine - especially if it is in accordance with His perfect will. I believed that it was God's perfect will that Howie and I remain together. I thought that the Bible instructed clearly that when two believers marry they should remain married no matter what.

I explained to Howie that I refused to let the boys be hurt. I told him my plan was to pretend as if nothing had happened when we were with the boys. If he let on and the boys got any hint that something was wrong I threatened that I would have no reason to stay with him. I made it clear that he shouldn't be fooled by the performance I would put on - to remember that I had been deeply hurt by his betrayal. I would have to act as though things were normal between Howie and me.

The day after I heard the news I had to go to an interview for a job. I didn't even want to climb out of bed, let alone see anyone. And yet, I had to make myself presentable and try to sell myself. All I remember of that interview is that the principal asked me if I usually talk so fast. I suppose my adrenaline was pumping as I worked so hard to focus on the answers to his questions. Thankfully, the Lord helped me through that stressful experience. I was able to return home and flop into bed.

The Lord helped me come up with creative excuses for my behavior. School had ended and it was summer vacation. It was typical for me to rest a lot so the boys wouldn't think it particularly odd for me to stay in bed (although I never usually stayed in bed for entire days!). We had been getting the house ready to sell so that we could move. We had just finished painting Chris's bedroom a cheery shade of peach and gotten a new carpet in there too. I asked Chris if we could trade rooms. He could sleep with Howie and I could sleep in his newly painted room until we moved. Chris liked the idea because he didn't like the smell of fresh paint.

It was the last week of August when I finally got a job. The Lord seems to like cliffhangers! Up until then we couldn't start trying to sell our house because we weren't certain we would be moving. I had only one week to select a school district for the boys, find a place for us to live, finish packing what we would need, buy a new car, and begin my new job. I had to take the boys to my mother's house. I shared the news about Howie and me with my mother, but asked that she not tell my father (because he was so sick with cancer). I told her that she could tell my aunt (who is my mother's identical twin sister). Other than that I didn't want to tell any other family members because I feared that the boys would sense something was wrong from them.

The townhouse I selected met most of our criteria. It was in a nice neighborhood, good school district, reasonable cost, near my new job, and near a train station (for Howie to get to work). They would not allow pets, however. That actually solved a problem for me. It gave me a good excuse to have Howie stay at our house (that we didn't yet sell) during the night. We explained to the boys that Howie had to stay at our old house with our dog over night. Howie stayed in our new house until the boys went to bed each night and then went to our old house. Then, first thing in the morning Howie drove to our new house so that the boys could see him before they went to school.

My way of coping with the broken promise was to immerse myself in God's Word. I searched for passages about marriage. At church one Sunday the pastor gave a message about divorce and marriage. He explained that God does permit a Christian to leave a Christian spouse in the case of infidelity. He went on to say that if the betrayed spouse decides to remain married, only the Lord could help that person forgive. So I knew that I needed to totally yield my emotions to Him and trust that He would help me forgive Howie.

Over the next five years some healing began to take place. Howie became more responsible with the boys. Up until then he had been mostly a friend to them. He began assuming responsibility for calling the school to work out a problem sometimes, going to school on Open House Nights, etc. He also began helping out with household chores more. He had always been very good about fixing things as soon as they needed to be fixed. I made an effort to continue to show respect to him. God blessed us with many happy times. But our marriage was far from being restored.

Often Howie would say things unkind to me. Usually it would be when he was impatient for some reason. In addition, he sometimes didn't pay attention to me when I was talking. Then, later, when I'd refer to something I'd said he would accuse me of never telling him. Finally I realized that most of his behavior was a result of him having ADHD. It was clear to me that he had ADHD. His report cards clearly painted the picture of a child who was impulsive, excessively talkative, and hyperactive. Then I realized God's wisdom in selecting me to be Howie's help mate. Since I was obsessively organized I had the skills to help my son and my husband learn the skills they needed to learn. So I shifted my thinking and gave up my resentment for having a husband who had those difficulties.

Lest I portray myself as the innocent victim in the marriage, I should point out that Howie had his hands full with me at times. Talking is what I do best, and Howie has learned to listen. Those who know me best probably pray extra hard for Howie!! Since I have a strong personality, I don't respond well to someone challenging me. Howie's gentle, easy-going personality perfectly compliments mine. He knows just how to handle me when I'm upset.

When Chris "got sick" (had his breakdown) Howie and I went to a few counseling sessions with one of our pastors, Marvin. Marvin was able to identify the heart of the problem. Howie was working to please me rather than to please God. Since Howie's efforts were driven by a motivation to make me happy, they ended whenever he perceived me to be happy. Sometimes Howie gave up trying altogether when he thought he couldn't make me happy. So there was no real commitment. Howie admitted he needed to treat me the way the Bible commands him to (as Christ loved the church), and that he needed to do it to please God.

My challenge was to continue to respect my husband and to trust God to rekindle my love for him. It took a tremendous step in faith sometimes just to talk to Howie. I was afraid that if I appeared too happy Howie would give up working on our relationship, and treat me casually. I was also afraid that if I tried to communicate with him he might hurt me again by not fully paying attention to me.

At the present time we are at a place in our marriage where we are just starting to rebuild on a firm foundation. We are both committed to allowing the Lord to lead us to be the husband or wife we need to be. We know that as long as we are yielded to His leading and committed to working on our relationship, God will restore our marriage. So, like most marriages, we are in the process of growing closer together. But as long as the Lord is central in our marriage I can have hope even without the evidence or feeling. It's a wonderful thing to have that assurance!

Chapter 20
A Final WORD (from God's Word)

Soon Chris will be finished his second year of college. In his junior year he'll be going farther away from home. He'll be attending the main campus of his college. We won't see him as often. With him about three and a half hours away, it won't be as easy for him to come home on the weekend. In his first two years of college there was a security in knowing that he was only about an hour away. I'm excited for Chris and thankful that he's well enough to go farther away, but I'm also mindful of the pressures he might face. As soon as fears begin to flood my mind with endless "what ifs", I immediately commit my thoughts and emotions to the Lord. Just as the Lord helped me through the worst of it so many times before, I've learned to remember Him. It helps to recall how He provided in the past in so many ways:

- He helped me have physical stamina.
- He helped me have wisdom.
- He helped me have emotional peace.
- He helped me have self control (in dealing with Chris or others).
- He helped me to forgive.
- He helped me to persevere and to endure.
- He helped me to focus at work even with a broken heart.
- He helped me find resources, knowledge, and professionals that could help him (or help us help him).
- He provided comfort.
- He provided wisdom and direction.
- He provided for practical and financial needs.
- He provided patience.
- He provided supportive friends.
- He provided joyful times and precious memories during the trials.

I remind myself that the trials I've experienced with Chris have prepared me to trust him with God.

If I've learned anything, however, I learned that I don't need to feel helpless. I can help Chris in several ways: I can allow him the opportunity to leave us and begin to walk with the Lord on his own. I can pray for him specifically and unceasingly. I can prepare myself mentally to be flexible should the Lord allow another U-turn in our lives (e. g., if Chris's rheumatoid arthritis continues to progress). I can prepare Chris by teaching him how to continue healthy habits on his own (to find out how to meet Christian friends who can support him, to find out how to contact resource people who would be trained to help him, etc.). I can remind Chris of the danger of the temptation to stop taking his medication. I can communicate with him regularly, sending him e-mail with encouraging Bible verses and words of support. I can demonstrate my faith in him by not pumping him regularly with questions about how he is doing. I can trust God to do what I can't (to keep Chris's mind and emotions strong).

Trusting God is easier said than done. That's why I've included some of the Bible verses (at the end of this chapter) that helped me in the past and those that I'll continue to lean on. But trusting God with my son is easier when I know that Chris has accepted Jesus as his Savior and is a child of God. It also becomes easier the more you know God.

Trusting people is even harder than trusting God. The people you trust the most are those who you know the best, who you believe love you, and who have demonstrated that their love is reliable and unconditional. But, human love is imperfect. Even those closest to you will let you down, betray you, or even reject you. God's Word tells us that all have sinned and that no one is perfect, no not one. Sometimes it's hard to even trust fellow Christians or family members. But with God's help we can have fulfilling relationships even after we experience someone's frailties. The Good News, however, is that there is One who can be trusted. There is One who won't reject us. There is One who has love for us that is unconditional, and that will never fail or never end. With God we never have to fear rejection or that we are unloved. We can have an assurance that He loves us, even when the world doesn't. That truth can be very real, very healing, and very encouraging to those who suffer from mental illness (or to those who have loved ones who suffer from mental illness).

I not only have a burden for those who are out of touch with reality due to mental illness, but I also have a burden for those who are out of touch with reality spiritually. There are people who have delusions that they have no need to have a personal relationship with Jesus. Frankly, I don't know if I would have survived my ordeal without the Lord in my life. True reality is this:

- Everyone will spend eternity either in heaven or hell.
- Jesus conquered sin and death on the cross.
- Anyone (no matter what religion) can accept the fact that Jesus died for their sin so that they can have everlasting life in heaven.
- Those who are saved also enjoy the power of the Comforter, the indwelling of the Holy Spirit, to help them through this life.
- You can have an abundant life filled with joy, peace, purpose, and hope when you have a daily walk with the Lord.

Chapter 21
Related Bible Verses

Note: All scripture quotations are taken from the New King James Version of the Bible.

Regarding The Mind:

"You will keep him in perfect peace, Whose mind is stayed on You, Because he trusts in You."

Isaiah 26:3

"For God has not given us a spirit of fear, but of power and of love and of a sound mind."

II Timothy 1:7

"Jesus said to him, 'You shall love the Lord your God with all your heart, with all your soul, and with your mind.'"

Matthew 22:37

"'And do not seek what you should eat or what you should drink, nor have an anxious mind."

Luke 12:29

"For to be carnally minded is death, but to be spiritually minded is life and peace."

Romans 8:6

"And do not be conformed to this world, but be transformed by the renewing of your mind, ..."

Romans 12:2

"For 'Who has known the mind of the Lord that he may instruct Him?' But we have the mind of Christ."

I Corinthians 2:16

"and the peace of God, which surpasses all understanding, will guard your hearts and minds through Christ Jesus."

Philippians 4:7

"Now, brethren, concerning the coming of our Lord Jesus Christ and our gathering together to Him, we ask you, not to be soon shaken in mind or troubled, either by spirit or by word or by letter, as if from us, as though the day of Christ had come."

II Thessalonians 2:1 & 2

Assuring Verses/Passages:

"In the multitude of my anxieties within me, Your comforts delight my soul."

Psalm 94:19

"When my spirit was overwhelmed within me, Then You knew my path. In the way in which I walk..."

Psalm 142:3

"He heals the brokenhearted and binds up their wounds."

Psalm 147:3

"I can do all things through Christ who strengthens me."

Philippians 4:13

"And my God shall supply all your need according to His riches in glory by Christ Jesus."

Philippians 4:19

"In the day when I cried out, You answered me, And made me bold with strength in my soul."

Psalm 138:3

"The Lord shall preserve you from all evil; He shall preserve your soul. The Lord shall preserve your going out and your coming in from this time forth, and even forevermore."

Psalm 121:7-8

Regarding Negative Feelings:

"Therefore my spirit is overwhelmed within me;
My heart within me is distressed.
Revive me, O Lord, for Your name's sake!
For Your righteousness' sake bring my soul out of trouble."

Psalm 143:4 & 11

"Therefore humble yourselves under the mighty hand of God, that He may exalt you in due time, casting all your care upon Him, for He cares for you. Be sober, be vigilant; because your adversary the devil walks about like a roaring lion, seeking whom he may devour. Resist him, steadfast in the faith, knowing that the same sufferings were experienced by your brotherhood in the world. But may the God of all grace, who called us to His eternal glory by Christ Jesus, after you have suffered a while, perfect, establish, strengthen, and settle you."

I Peter 5:7

What To Do When Feeling Overwhelmed:

"Be anxious for nothing, but in everything by prayer and supplication, with thanksgiving, let your requests be made known to God;

Philippians 4:6

"I cried out to God with my voice — To God with my voice; And He gave ear to me. In the day of my trouble I sought the Lord: My hand was stretched out in the night without ceasing; My soul refused to be comforted. I remembered God, and was troubled; I complained, and my spirit was overwhelmed. You hold my eyelids open; I am so troubled that I cannot speak. I have considered the days of old, The years of ancient times. I call to remembrance my song in the night; I meditate within my heart, And my spirit makes diligent search. Will the Lord cast off forever? And will He be favorable no more? Has His mercy ceased forever? Has His promise failed forevermore? Has God forgotten to be gracious? Has He in anger shut up His tender mercies? Selah And I said, 'This is my anguish; But I will remember the years of the right hand of the Most High.' I will remember the works of the Lord; Surely I still remember Your wonders of old. I will also meditate on all Your work, And talk of Your deeds. Your way, O God, is in the sanctuary; Who is so great a God as our God? You are the God who does wonders;"

Psalm 77:1-14a

"Hear my cry, O God; Attend to my prayer. From the end of the earth I will cry to You, When my heart is overwhelmed; Lead me to the rock that is higher than I."

Psalm 61:1 & 2

"Cast your burden on the Lord, And He shall sustain you; He shall never permit the righteous to be moved."

Psalm 55:22

"Why are you cast down, O my soul? And why are you disquieted within me? Hope in God; For I shall yet praise Him, The help of my countenance and my God."

Psalm 42:11

For Those in Danger or Perceived Danger, For Those Suffering from Depression and Paranoia):

Psalm 31:1-24 (the entire chapter) Recommended daily reading!

For Comfort & Hope For Those Suffering, and For Those Who Are Ministering to Someone Who Is Suffering:

Psalm 34:1-22 (the entire chapter) Recommended daily reading!

Encouragement For Those Who Are Caring For Someone Who Is Mentally Ill:

"Yet in all these things we are more than conquerors through Him who loved us."

Romans 8:37

"Concerning this thing I pleaded with the Lord three times that it might depart from me. And He said to me, 'My grace is sufficient for you, for My strength is made perfect in weakness.' Therefore most gladly I will rather boast in my infirmities, that the power of Christ may rest upon me."

II Corinthians 12:8 & 9

"For we do not wrestle against flesh and blood, but against principalities, against powers, against the rulers of the darkness of this age, against spiritual hosts of wickedness in the heavenly places. Therefore take up the whole armor of God, that you may be able to withstand in the evil day, and having done all to stand. And take the helmet of salvation, and the sword of the Spirit, which is the word of God;   praying always with all prayer and supplication in the Spirit, being watchful to this end with all perseverance and supplication for all the saints-"

Ephesians 6:12, 13, & 18

"We then who are strong ought to bear with the cruples (weaknesses) of the weak, and not to please ourselves. Now may the God of hope fill you with all joy and peace in believing, that you may abound in hope by the power of the Holy Spirit."

Romans 15:1 & 13

PART TWO

Chapter 22
Information and Help

There are many excellent books on the market that provide detailed information about Attention Deficit Hyperactivity Disorder (ADHD), Tourette Syndrome, mental illness, and Post-Traumatic Stress Disorder. Therefore, mostly general information will be provided in this section. This book is not intended to be an all-inclusive, exhaustive medical resource. Many people struggling with mental illness, or with a loved one with mental illness may be overwhelmed with life as it is; there would be no point in overwhelming the reader with endless information.

Since this book was written to help you along your journey, it will point you in the direction you need to go to begin your investigation for help and support. Each reader's journey will include slightly different paths because each person's situation and experiences are unique. That is why you will find road signs instead of exact addresses. In other words, you will be given the name of an excellent catalog rather than a long list of recommended books. Then you can use that catalog to locate books that suit your needs.

In the context of sharing information about conditions listed in this autobiography (especially ADHD), it is important to point out how the current popular thinking plays a role in accuracy of information. When my son was first diagnosed with ADHD in 1985 most people had never heard of the disorder. Fifteen years later it is not only a household word but many people are tired of hearing that someone has a child diagnosed with ADHD. It is no wonder that people have grown skeptical about the diagnosis. There is a growing intolerance for accepting any information about ADHD for several reasons:

- Sometimes children are misdiagnosed. In other words there is an over diagnosis; some children are diagnosed with ADHD who really do not have the disorder.

- In other cases parents feel that if their child has the diagnosis then they are off the hook and not responsible to help their child learn the skills that they must learn (social skills, organizational skills, ways to compensate for difficulties with attention, etc.). In those cases the parents aren't necessarily bad parents, but rather parents who believe that having the disorder makes it impossible for their child to learn necessary life skills.

- Some people attempt to use the disorder as an excuse for inappropriate behavior. It is very frustrating for a teacher to hear a parent say something like, "I'm sorry that Joey constantly interrupts in class, but he has ADHD." It is difficult for children with ADHD to learn to control impulses, but adults can teach those children how to compensate (by asking for breaks to run errands, by using a silent timer on his desk to keep him focused for a specific time period, etc.)

- There are strong popular feelings about medication. It is not politically correct to use medication for children who have behavior problems. In addition, the treatment of choice sometimes is a "more natural" treatment.

At the risk of sounding preachy and politically incorrect, I must emphasize that medication is an effective treatment for ADHD (when used in conjunction with family counseling that teaches strategies). Since so many children (and adults) have used medication for ADHD for literally decades, we have proof of the success of the treatment. Many independent research studies have been done that include longitudinal studies (effects over time). Yes, there are risks, but there are risks to taking any medication. When prescribed and monitored by a knowledgeable physician, bad side effects can be prevented. The rule of thumb is to try one full year of treatment without medication (after a correct diagnosis of ADHD is made) and also provide family counseling and behavior strategies. If, after the year, the behavior of the child is not manageable (according to all the adults who manage him), then medication should be seriously considered as part of the treatment. Whenever medication is prescribed parents should always remember that, "You don't give the pill without teaching the skills."

Considering the current popular thinking, it is critical that adults consider the source when obtaining information. Friends, teachers, physicians, the internet, books, and magazines can all be good or bad sources. Each source can provide either accurate or biased and inaccurate information. Any information should be based on sound research. The key to being informed is to carefully select your source and use several good sources. In my case, even our physicians have given correct and incorrect information. Therefore, it is important to consistently seek accurate, research-based information. National organizations are the best place to find current and accurate information. They can also lead you to literature and physicians who can provide accurate information. If your source has not read recent research, then consider that you might be receiving their opinion or misinformation rather than fact. The more you do your homework the better an advocate you can be for your loved one.

To completely understand one form of mental illness, related laws, or Attention Deficit Hyperactivity Disorder, you should go beyond the general information that is shared in this portion of the book. Partial knowledge can sometimes lead to misunderstanding or confusion. So read on and learn more.

Chapter 23
Where to Find Accurate Information

Recommended Catalogs:
For ADHD: The *A.D.D. WareHouse* is the most extensive listing of books and resources available regarding ADHD. There are entire sections for parents, adults, and kids.
The address and phone numbers are:

    A. D. D. WareHouse
    300 Northwest 70th Avenue, Suite 102
    Plantation, FL 33317
    1-954-792-8944 or 1-800-233-9273
    www.addwarehouse.com

Catalogs For Gifted: Prufrock *Press* includes several suggested magazines and journals. In addition, there are resource books and an extensive variety of books to challenge the gifted learner. The address and phone numbers are:

    Prufrock Press
    P. O. Box 8813
    Waco, TX 76714-8813
    1-800-998-2208
    http://www.prufrock.com.

Recommended Organizations:
For ADHD, Gifted, and Mental Illness:

The Council for Exceptional Children
1920 Association Drive
Reston, Virginia 20191-1589
1-888-CEC-SPED (or 1-888-232-7733)
1-800-232-7323
http://www.cec.sped.org

More Recommended Organizations:

Large city hospitals can be a tremendous resource. They either provide their own information, or can point you in the right direction to get more information. One example is the Children's Seashore House in Philadelphia, PA. They publish a resource directory called *Special Kids*. It includes local and national organizations, local special schools and day care facilities, and information about legislation, advocacy groups, early intervention, camps, bilingual services, and more. They also publish *Metro Kids*. For information contact them at:

> *Metro Kids* Magazine
> 1080 N. Delaware Avenue
> Suite 702
> Philadelphia, PA 19125
> 1-215-291-5560 or 1-609-667-3555

More Recommended Organizations:
For Mental Illness:

National Alliance for the Mentally Ill
Colonial Place Three
2107 Wilson Blvd., Suite 300
Arlington, VA 22201-3042
www.nami.org

National Institutes of Mental Health
Room 7C-02, 5600 Fishers Land
Rockville, MD 20857
1-301-443-4513
http://www.nihm.nih.gov/publicat/adhd.htm

Focus on the Family (for Christian literature and information)
Colorado Springs, CO 80995
1-800-A-FAMILY (or 1-800-232-6459)   www.family.org
More Recommended Organizations:
Additional Organizations for ADHD and Mental Illness:
The National Information Center for Children and Youth with Disabilities
PO Box 1492
Washington, DC 20013-1492
1-800-695-0285

For ADHD:
Children and Adults with Attention Deficit Disorder (CHADD)
499 NW 70th Avenue
Suite 109
Plantation, FL 33317
1-954-587-3700 or fax 1-954-587-4599
www.chadd.org
(Your local chapter should be found in your telephone book.)

National Attention Deficit Disorder Association
PO Box 972
Mentor, OH 44061-0972
1-800-487-2282 or 1-216-350-9595
www.add.org
For Tourette Syndrome:
Tourette Syndrome Association
42-40 Bell Blvd., Suite 205
Bayside, NY 11361
1-888-4TOURET or 1-718-224-2999

How to Locate Support Groups:

There are many secular support groups for parents of children with ADHD or adults with ADHD. You can find a listing of them in your local newspaper, hospitals, or you can call national organizations, such as Children and Adults with Attention Deficit Disorder (CHADD), to find out local meeting locations and times. Many Christians find those support groups helpful only for information. Secular support groups cannot offer the hope that we can only find in Jesus Christ. Christian support groups are fewer and more difficult to find. Contact your local church or any large local church to find Christian support groups. Christian support groups for parents of children with any type of special need would provide the support that you need. No matter what type of disorder or handicap your child has you experience the same feelings of despair, helplessness, confusion, loneliness, and uncertainty. Good Christian support groups will remind you of God's love, faithfulness, power, and provision.

Chapter 24
Recommended Books and Resources

Resource Books:

    The few books listed here are my personal favorites. They were selected because they are relatively short, easy to read, practical, accurate, and up-to-date. All of the books listed may be found in and ordered from the *A. D. D. WareHouse* catalog (address provided earlier in Part Two).

Taking Charge of ADHD: The Complete, Authoritative Guide for Parents, by Russell A. Barkley, Ph. D.

The ADD Hyperactivity Workbook for Parents, Teachers, and Kids, by Harvey C. Parker, Ph. D.

About Attention Deficit Disorder, Published by Channing L. Bete Co., Inc.

A Parent's Guide: Attention Deficit Hyperactivity Disorder in Children, by Sam Goldstein, Ph. D. and Michael Goldstein, M. D.

Children with Tourette Syndrome: A Parent's Guide, Edited by Tracy Haerie

Making the Grade: An Adolescent's Struggle with ADD, by Roberta N. Parker

I Would If I Could: A Teenager's Guide to ADHD/Hyperactivity, by Michael Gordon, Ph. D.

Skillstreaming the Elementary School Child: New Strategies and Perspectives for Teaching Prosocial Skills and Skillstreaming the

Adolescent: New Strategies and Perspectives for Teaching Prosocial Skills, by Dr. Ellen McGinnis and Dr. Arnold P. Goldstein

Medications for Attention Disorders (ADHD/ADD) and Related Medical Problems: A Comprehensive Handbook, by Edna D. Copeland, Ph. D., and Steven C. Copps, M. D.

Related Christian Autobiographies:

When You Can't Come Back: A Story of Courage and Grace, by Dave and Jan Dravecky

A Joy I'd Never Known, by Jan Dravecky
Stormie - A Story of Forgiveness and Healing, by Stormie Omartian

Christian Self-Help Books:

Telling Yourself the Truth, by William Backus and Marie Chapian

Stomping Out the Darkness, by Neil T. Anderson and Dave Park

Dark Clouds Silver Linings, by Dr. Archibald D. Hart

How to Help a Heartbroken Friend, by David Biebel

Secular Self-Help Book:

I Can't Get Over It - A Handbook for Trauma Survivors, by Aphrodite Matsakis, Ph. D.

Other Resources:
Audio tapes regarding ADHD and mental illness are available from Focus on the Family.

A Final Word:

There are many other excellent books. Search beyond this list.

Chapter 25
Related Laws

General Information:

In order to find information regarding related laws quickly and easily, you can locate numerous sites on the internet. Begin your search by typing 'special education law' or 'laws for disabled.' One source I located that way was a special education advocacy web site called 'Wrightslaw' found at http.//www.wrightslaw.com. Other ways you can obtain information about laws related to mental illness is by going to your local library or by calling your local representatives. In addition, you may obtain more information about federal laws regarding individuals with disabilities from the federal government's Equal Employment Opportunity Commission (EEOC, 1-800-669-EEOC) and the President's Commission on the Employment of Persons with Disabilities (1-202-376-6200).

Americans with Disabilities Act (ADA):

The ADA was signed into law on July 26, 1990 with the intention of making all aspects of American society more accessible to people with disabilities. The law is divided into five titles:

Title I - Employment:

Business must provide reasonable accommodations to protect the rights of individuals with disabilities in all aspects of employment. Possible accommodations might include restructuring jobs, altering the layout of workstations, or modifying equipment. Employment aspects may include the application process, hiring, wages, benefits, and all other aspects of employment. Medical examinations are highly regulated.

Title II - Public Service:

Public services, which include state and local government instrumentalities, the National Railroad Passenger Corporation, and other commuter authorities, cannot deny services to people with disabilities participation in programs or activities which are available to people without disabilities. In addition, public transportation systems, such as public transit buses, must be accessible to individuals with disabilities.

Title III - Public Accommodations:

All new construction and existing public structures must be accessible to individuals with disabilities. For existing facilities, barriers to services must be removed if readily achievable. Public accommodations include facilities such as restaurants, hotels, grocery stores, retail stores, etc., as well as privately owned transportation systems.

Title IV - Telecommunications:

Telecommunications companies offering telephone service to the general public must have telephone relay service to individuals who use telecommunication devices for the deaf (TTYs or similar devices).

Title V - Miscellaneous:

This section of the law includes a provision prohibiting either (a) coercing or threatening or (b) retaliating against the disabled or those attempting to aid people with disabilities in asserting their rights under the ADA.

Individuals with Disabilities Education Act (IDEA):

This law was first implemented in 1975 as PL 94-142. At that time approximately a million children with disabilities were excluded from schools and denied appropriate services. Formerly, ninety percent of children with developmental disabilities were previously housed in state institutions. The rationale for this law was that all children are entitled to free and appropriate public education (known as FAPE) in the least restrictive environment.

The law addresses every detail of the educational process for children with special needs. It specifies: services provided, duration of services, amount of time services are provided, assessment methods, current education levels, goals, parental involvement, ratio of students being served to adults, categories of disabilities, criteria for exit from services, timelines, an individualized education plan (IEP), etc.

Section 504:

In the 1995 July/August edition of Learning Disabilities News briefs Section 504 was described this way: "Section 504 does not in any way require that standards be lowered. Rather, the intention of Section 504, since it is civil rights legislation, is to remove barriers so that persons with disabilities can fully participate in activities. In the case of persons with learning disabilities, the term barrier does not just refer to physical barriers but also programmatic and organizational barriers. Thus, reasonable adjustments or accommodations must be made when the means of instruction or testing prevents or limits participation for a person with disabilities.

"For example, mandating that all testing must be done in the same way is discriminatory against a wide range of persons with disabilities. Therefore, Section 504 requires that testing of people with disabilities be given in the format that will allow students with disabilities to best show their capacity to complete the assigned tasks."

The article went on to clarify when accommodations are required. They said, "However, documentation must be in place to show the disability and that accommodations are really necessary to allow students to show their true capacities."

When this law was enacted in 1973 it specified that no qualified individual with disabilities in the United States shall be denied the benefits of, be excluded from the participation in, or be subjected to discrimination under any program or activity receiving federal financial assistance based solely on his or her disability. Section 504 differs from IDEA in several ways:

- It defines free and appropriate public education more broadly to include in-class accommodations for those children with learning needs who do not qualify for special education.
- Rather than meeting one of thirteen specific categories of disabilities, the child must meet the definition of functional impairment, which substantially limits a major life activity, such as learning and communication.
- Section 504 does not require a written Individualized Education Plan (IEP), but it does require that a plan be developed and put into place. It does not have the same requirements of the plan specified in IDEA.

Every district is required to have a Section 504 officer who is responsible for assuring district compliance.

Chapter 26
Mental Illness

What is mental illness?

The term 'mental illness' is misleading. It implies that there are illnesses that affect only the mind. The fact is that those illnesses that we call physical illnesses are often related to mental illnesses (and vice versa). The term 'mental illness' also implies that it is something different than physical illness. If people could view mental illness as they do physical illness, there would be fewer stigmas attached to it and less misunderstanding.

According to the *Diagnostic and Statistical Manual of Mental Disorders - Fourth Edition (DSM-IV)* , a mental disorder is defined as, "a clinically significant behavioral or psychological syndrome or pattern that occurs in an individual and that is associated with present distress (e. g., a painful symptom) or disability (i. e., impairment in one or more important areas of functioning) or with a significantly increased risk of suffering death, pain, disability, or an important loss of freedom. In addition, this syndrome or pattern must not be merely an expectable and culturally sanctioned response to a particular event, for example, the death of a loved one. Whatever its original cause, it must currently be considered a manifestation of a behavioral, psychological, or biological dysfunction in the individual."

Mental illness is a very broad term. Mental disorders are currently classified into the following six categories:
- Mental disorders due to a general medical condition
- Substance-induced disorders
- Psychotic disorders
- Mood disorders
- Anxiety disorders
- Somatoform disorders (the presence of physical symptoms that suggest a general medical condition, but are not fully explained by a general medical condition, by the direct effects

of a substance, or by another mental disorder) Example: hypochondria

It is important to note that psychosocial and environmental problems (such as a negative life event, inadequate social support, or family stress) may affect the diagnosis, treatment, and prognosis of mental disorders.

Mental disorders might be identified as mild, moderate, or severe. In addition, a disorder might be identified as in partial remission, in full remission, or a prior history.

Treatment:

The nature and severity of the disorder will dictate the appropriate treatment. A psychiatrist will determine the necessary treatment. It cannot be emphasized enough that there are medical treatments available for mental disorders that are organic. With more brain research there are many options today that offer hope to individuals who suffer from brain chemical imbalances or deficiencies. Another point that should be stressed is that, regardless of the disorder, the individual's mental health, physical health, and emotional health all should be addressed. That will translate into recommendations from a team of professionals. The physician might recommend a nutrition plan; a psychologist might recommend strategies (e.g., setting boundaries, keeping a journal), and a psychiatrist might recommend medication.

As we learned, if medication is the recommended treatment, there are several ways to adjust the medication. It might be necessary to use a combination of medications, to change a medication (e. g., if a person's body chemistry suddenly changes and one medication no longer is effective), to slightly adjust the dosage of a medication (e. g., at a stressful time of day), or to change the time of day the medication is administered (e. g., administering medication in the evening to reduce drowsy side effects). This information is shared because it is encouraging to know that nowadays there are many options available for individuals who are being treated medically for mental illness. No adjustments, however, should ever be made without the recommendation of a physician or psychiatrist.

Another important point about medication is that it can be indicated for either a long period or brief period of time. A psychiatrist or physician will monitor a patient and determine the recommended duration for a specific disorder.

What is a Biblical model for dealing with mental illness?

No matter what condition a person suffers, he or she still has the same human nature and spiritual needs as anyone else. Physical, mental, and emotional treatment should take place in the context of spiritual truths. They include:

- God is close to the broken-hearted. (Isaiah 61:1, Psalm 147:3)
- He is with us in our suffering and He has a purpose in it. He works all things together for good to those who love Him and who are called according to His purpose. (Romans 8:28, II Corinthians 1:3-7)
- God has sent the Comforter. He promised to never leave us or forsake us. (John 14:16, Acts 9:31, II Corinthians 1:4, II Corinthians 7:6, Hebrews 13:5)
- It is God's desire for us to have joy. We can find abundant joy not in others, but in Him. (Romans 15:13)
- God is faithful to His promises. If we turn to Him, He will provide all that we need. (Philippians 4:19)
- God will protect our heart and mind. (Philippians 4:7)
- God provides strength. He is strong when we are weak. (Psalm 55:22, II Corinthians 12:9)
- God can renew our mind and give us a new eternal perspective. (II Corinthians 4:16-18, James 1:2-12) In all things we are more than conquerors. (Romans 8:35-39)
- God hears us. (Psalm 66:19, I John 5:14)

Treatment for the mentally ill must include an emphasis on those truths so that there can be renewed thinking. All of us, at times, struggle because of our wrong thinking and motives (that come from the evil desires of our heart). Such wrong thinking influences our actions. For example, if we think it is most important to please others we might experience paralyzing fear if we have to do a speech in public. It is only when we shift our focus to pleasing God that we find peace in those types of situations. Any wrong thinking can exacerbate symptoms of a mental disorder. Renewed thinking can help them see their situations in life in a new way. Those who suffer from any form of mental illness (or from any affliction, for that matter) need hope. That hope can be found in Him and in His Word. It is in God's Word that we can find real peace.

Therefore, the Biblical model for dealing with mental illness is to draw near to God and to find hope in His Word. In doing that we can have renewed thinking, viewing our situations in light of God's power and love.

Chapter 27
Attention Deficit Hyperactivity Disorder

Definition of ADHD:

According to the Diagnostic and Statistical Manual of Mental Disorders - *Fourth Edition (DSM-IV)*, ADHD is characterized as, "a persistent pattern of inattention and/or hyperactivity-impulsivity that is more frequent and severe than is typically observed in individuals at a comparable level of development. Some hyperactive-impulsive or inattentive symptoms that cause impairment must have been present before age 7 years, although many individuals are diagnosed after the symptoms have been present for a number of years. Some impairment from the symptoms must be present in at least two settings (e. g., at home and at school or work). There must be clear evidence of interference with developmentally appropriate social, academic, or occupational functioning. The disturbance does not occur exclusively during the course of a Pervasive Developmental Disorder, Schizophrenia, or other Psychotic Disorder and is not better accounted for by another mental disorder (e. g., a Mood Disorder, Anxiety Disorder, Dissociative Disorder, or Personality Disorder)."

History of ADHD:

During the twentieth century ADHD was known by several different names. Each name reflected the current conceptualization of the disorder.

The different names included:
- A Defect in Moral Control - coined by the British physician George Still in 1902,
- Minimal brain dysfunction - MBD - coined in the first half of the twentieth century (introducing the neurological basis for the patterns of behavior frequently associated with ADHD, without defining characteristics of the behaviors),

- The Hyperkinetic Reaction of Childhood - coined in the middle of the twentieth century (with the emphasis then on hyperactivity as the primary problem)
- ADD with or without Hyperactivity - coined in 1980,
- ADHD - coined in the late 1980s,
- ADHD, Predominantly Inattentive Type, ADHD, Predominantly Hyperactive-Impulsive Type, ADHD, Combined Type - coined in 1994

The very latest perspective is to view ADHD as Executive Dysfunction. This perspective adds more dignity to the diagnosis because it correctly puts the emphasis back on the brain dysfunction that is involved rather than on the behavior. As long as the term for the diagnosis included a term related to behavior (hyperactivity), there was a tendency to view people with ADHD as having a flaw in their character - having a problem of their will rather with their brain chemistry.

To understand the Executive Dysfunction, you must understand the Executive Function of the brain. On March 30, 1989 at a seminar of the National Association of School Psychologists in Boston, Massachusetts, Dennis Williams (of the Good Samaritan Neuropsychological Services in Washington) presented this new perspective on ADHD. He explained that the Executive Function processes are basically what are necessary for activities essential for survival. The Executive Function of the brain is what helps us direct our attention, recognize goals, formulate intentions, make plans for attainment of goals, execute plans to achieve a purpose, and recognize attainment of goals. All tasks we do incorporate executive function processes. If the Executive Function is intact, we are able to spontaneously and independently begin and complete tasks.

In contrast, Executive Dysfunction involves the following disturbances to those abilities (listed above):

- An ability to verbalize appropriate action, but difficulty in carrying out the appropriate action (a child can tell you what he should do, but has trouble consistently doing it)
- An inability to generalize, or limited carryover (a child can behave in one particular situation, with one specific person, but cannot transfer that ability to another similar situation with a different adult)
- A limited awareness of deficits or lack of awareness of problems
- A tendency to be distracted by irrelevant stimuli (a child might distract himself, or be distracted by other people or things in the environment)
- A disruption in the execution of or memory for routines

Dennis Williams also listed other hallmarks of the Executive Dysfunction. Those included: perseveration (doing or saying something repeatedly), failure to initiate appropriate activity, failure to maintain effort, failure to recognize and/or utilize feedback, and failure to modulate (regulate or adjust) activity without cues.

It is evident that children with ADHD exhibit those behaviors specified by Dennis Williams. Perhaps ADHD will soon be referred to as Executive Dysfunction. Regardless of whether or not the name changes again, this new perspective offers new insight into how to help individuals with those difficulties and behavior patterns.

Causes of ADHD:

To date, no one can say with certainty what is the cause of ADHD. However, there is a theory that is most widely accepted. It is the theory that ADHD is an inherited neurobiological disorder. According to the neurobiological disorder theory, there is a deficiency of the neurotransmitter chemicals in the brain. The job of the neurotransmitter chemicals is to send sensory information to millions of nerve cells in the brain. Those chemicals have been found to be directly responsible for behavior, emotion, and cognition in animals and humans.

There are other suspected causes of ADHD that are accepted as possible causes. Since ADHD tends to run in families, there seems to be a hereditary link. Therefore, it appears ADHD might be genetic, in some cases. In other cases the disorder may be a result of a known prior disease, an acquired head injury, neurological damage resulting from a birth injury during pregnancy or labor and delivery, or being born to a mother who abused alcohol or drugs during pregnancy.

It is important to mention several factors that are believed to cause ADHD, but have no scientific evidence. They include diet, food allergies, infections, inner ear disorders, and child rearing practices. Of those unsubstantiated beliefs, the belief that poor parenting causes ADHD is the most damaging to parents. Parents with children who have ADHD feel very isolated, inadequate, frustrated, and discouraged. When uninformed people imply or say that the cause of their child's behavior is poor parenting, parents unnecessarily feel humiliated, ashamed and guilty. Parents of children with ADHD need to be supported rather than judged. In many cases I have found that parents of children with ADHD should be applauded because they work harder as parents and persevere against all odds (sometimes without significant results) - out of their love and dedication for their children. Like many parents of children with special needs, my husband and I were not able to date for several years. We were not able to find baby sitters that would be able to lovingly manage our son and his brother.

Diagnosing ADHD:

A word about this information: Since I became a special education teacher 25 years ago I have heard countless stories about how children have been diagnosed with ADHD. Sometimes children are misdiagnosed or go undiagnosed because the evaluation wasn't thorough enough. There are several reasons why a thorough evaluation must be done:

- Behavior is extremely complex.
- One specific behavior such as trouble following directions can be indicative of several different causes: a hearing problem, a language problem, a more general learning disability, an auditory processing problem, an undetermined illness, lack of self-confidence or shyness, ADHD, a symptom of abuse, an emotional problem, etc.
- Problematic behavior will not be observed in one setting and yet be present in another setting (e. g., hyperactivity might not be observed when a child is watching TV or playing a computer game, but it might always be a problem when there are more distractions in situations like birthday parties, sports activities, recess, and Sunday school).
- Different caregivers can offer important insight about the child that others haven't observed (even mothers notice things about their child that fathers might not have the opportunities to notice).
- Reactions to behavior can be very subjective.
- Trained professionals can help confirm or eliminate causes (e. g., a physician can eliminate the possibility of any other health problem, and a teacher can help confirm ADHD by offering very objective observations of the child in comparison to other children and in the context of routine classroom activities with other children).

Therefore, it is important to use a multidisciplinary approach to determine whether or not an individual has ADHD. In other words, it is critical that considering information from the parents, school personnel, the primary physician, and a professional who is knowledgeable about ADHD (such as a psychologist, a psychiatrist, or a neurologist) make the diagnosis. The primary physician most likely will not be able to make an accurate diagnosis based solely on an office visit because of the very nature of the environment (being relatively quiet and structured). The best way to go about determining whether or not a child has ADHD is to have a neuropsychological evaluation done and then share the results with the primary physician. Many people have a psychological evaluation done by either a psychologist or a psychiatrist. But a neurologist who specializes in the brain would do a neuropsychological evaluation. This is not to say that it is less effective to have a psychologist or a psychiatrist administer a psychological evaluation. I merely suggested a neurologist because parents often ask me what would be the best way to go. Either way, it is critical that the evaluation includes a developmental history, a thorough physical examination, and checklists and interviews with the teachers and parents.

Treatment - Medication:

At the risk of oversimplifying the neurophysiology of ADHD, I offer this brief explanation. According to the current theory of ADHD, it is believed that people with ADHD have insufficient amounts of dopamine. Dopamine is the chemical in the brain that appears to play a major role in things like attention and inhibition. In order to get normal levels of attention and inhibition, you have to produce normal levels of dopamine.

But if the brain does not produce normal levels of dopamine, then medication offers an alternative. There are other disorders that are treated effectively by medication - a synthetic version of what the body should produce. Many people with diabetes or thyroid problems would not survive if they didn't take medication that provided what their bodies didn't produce. Likewise, individuals with ADHD can benefit from medication that helps their brain function.

Although medication has proven to be an effective treatment for ADHD for decades, many people are Ritalin phobic. Books such as *Ritalin Nation* and *Running on Ritalin* contribute to the misinformation that drives peoples' fears of using medication to treat ADHD. If one would collect all the sound research studies that have been done to prove the effectiveness of medication, an entire book could be written. But in this age of natural approaches and supplements, a book such as that might not sell. Popular beliefs, however, cannot change the facts. The fact is that medication is a powerful and successful treatment for ADHD. The fact is that individuals with ADHD who are not treated with medication are at greater risk for drug abuse. Nora Volkow, the chairman of medicine at Brookhaven National Laboratory, says that between ten and twenty percent of drug addicts have ADHD. She said that, "In studies, when they were given Ritalin they would stop taking cocaine." Timothy Wilens, a psychiatrist at Harvard Medical School presented data at a National Institutes of Health conference on ADHD which showed that treating children with ADHD with Ritalin and similar medications lowered the risk of their developing drug problems in adolescence by an extraordinary sixty-eight percent.

The simple fact that most people only think of Ritalin when they think of medication for ADHD demonstrates how little the general population knows about effective treatments for ADHD. Medications for Attention Disorders (ADHD/ADD) and Related Medical Problems is a 406-page book listing numerous options of medication (Ritalin being only one option). In that comprehensive handbook this reluctance to use medications for ADHD is addressed:

"For at least fifty years, parents, teachers and pediatricians have been aware of this group of children and adolescents who are unmanageable at home and unsuccessful at school. For at least that long diverse treatment approaches have been tried and discarded. When one examines the medical literature, one is struck with the fact that one treatment approach appears consistently, for over fifty years, to have been helpful with this group, that is, the use of stimulant medications. From the vast array of research data at this time, one can safely say that medication is an appropriate and effective intervention for at least three fourths of those diagnosed with physiologic ADHD/ADD. Recent researchers suggest that as many as 90% may be assisted (Calis et al., 1990)

"Despite the impressive track record of medications, people are, nevertheless, uneasy about giving medication to children and adolescents, especially medicines which affect brain functioning. They are even more uneasy about giving it, presumably, *to control behavior*. Most do not understand the neurophysiology of ADHD/ADD and thus do not realize that medication is not doing anything *to the child*, but rather acting as a normalizer of brain functioning, so that the child, adolescent or adult can function normally.... How many of us would deny the diabetic child insulin or the adolescent with hypothyroidism, thyroxin?"

For detailed information about medication as a treatment for ADHD I recommend <u>Medications for Attention Disorders (ADHD/ADD) and Related Medical Problems</u> . It truly is a comprehensive guide for understanding ADHD, causes, treatments, and related disorders. There are several general points that I'd like to mention regarding medication:

1)   Since we are all unique, medical treatment has to be customized to individual conditions. Different people with ADHD have different statures and different levels of dopamine. Therefore different people require different dosages of medication. In addition, side effects will vary from person to person. Hence, the need to be treated by a physician who is knowledgeable about medical treatment of ADHD.

2)   Be informed. Make it your mission to know all there is to know in current research about the medication that is being taken for ADHD. (Refer to the section in Part Two entitled 'Where to Find Accurate Information.')

3)   Since medication can have dramatic effects with children who are extremely hyperactive, the change in behavior can be startling.

Some parents feel that their child has become lethargic from the medication. In actuality, the child has simply become more calm and manageable.

4)   Stimulant medications do not stunt growth.

5)   Individuals with tics or Tourette Syndrome should not be concerned about taking stimulant drugs. It is the opinion of many experts in the field that if the ADHD is an important problem to target, the stimulant drugs need not be withheld, even if there is a risk (in a minority of cases) that the tics might become worse. There seems little, if any, indication that such worsening is permanent. If, however, the tics do become significantly worse, then a clinical choice would have to be made to: (a) tolerate the tics (as a lesser problem); (b) suppress the tics with an anti-tic medication; (c) try a different class of drug for the ADHD (such as antidepressants or antihypertensives); or (d) a combination of medications (one to treat the ADHD and one to treat the tics).

Adults With ADHD (also know as ADHD-residual type):

My husband's first-hand account of what it's like to be an adult with ADHD is obviously missing. That was unavoidable. It is both significant and common (but not always the case) for men to deny that they have ADHD. Although my husband's difficulties with attention and organization impact all the family members, he simply doesn't see any problems. No matter how many times he misplaces or loses something, he doesn't accept that his organizational difficulties are just one symptom of ADHD. Howie has been open and willing to suggestions of ways he can deal with one specific problem, but until just lately he has not been able to admit that he has ADHD. Often when he asks someone a question he impulsively and impatiently expresses his frustration or assumes the person has chosen not to respond. When I pointed it out to him he said he wasn't aware that he was doing that. I asked him to see if he did that with his co-workers. He realized that it was a problem. Then I suggested that he simply count to ten in his mind while he waits for someone to process and respond to a question. It is my opinion that Howie won't accept that he has ADHD because then he will feel that he is less of a man. I've even had discussions with him saying, "Can't you see that you are a wonderful man who happens to have ADHD?" And he responded with a smile saying, "Yes, I know I'm a wonderful man."

Is it so important for him to acknowledge that he has ADHD? Not unless he doesn't take responsibility for the difficulties that he has. For example, I've always encouraged him to ask me (or someone else) what he could do to compensate for some difficulty that he has related to ADHD. Sometimes he's pretty good about that. I remember when he was the church treasurer. Sitting at the dining room table buried in mountains of files, bills, and papers he asked me to help him get organized. At that point it was impossible to find out his 'system' and fix it. It was easier for me to help him begin from there using an organized system of color-coded file folders (once he told me the categories of bills). Other times, however, he is not as responsible and it impacts me negatively. For example, sometimes I don't realize that he is not paying attention to me when I am telling him something important. Later, when he finds out the information he blames me for not telling him sooner.

Although Howie has trouble accepting that he has ADHD, he does accept some responsibility for his needs. His response
is sort of middle-of-the-road. You can find adults who totally accept it and others who deny it totally. I have met adults (men and women) with ADHD who are able to accept that they simply have a medical condition and take steps to help themselves. On the other end of the scale I know some adults who completely deny their ADHD and who make no attempts to develop good life skills. They suffer tremendous losses (loss of a job or loss of a spouse).

In 1992 Devin R. Murphy, Ph. D (from the University of Massachusetts Medical Center) wrote about 'Coping Strategies for ADHD Adults.' He explained, "The symptoms that occur in adults in type and severity and can cause significant impairments in interpersonal relations, marriage, emotional well being, employment, as well as in daily adaptive functioning. Despite their symptoms, some ADHD adults have learned to successfully compensate for their difficulties and function very well. However, most ADHD adults are restless, easily distracted, have trouble focusing, concentrating, and sustaining attention, are impulsive and impatient, have inconsistent work performance, are often unorganized and fail to plan ahead, often fail to finish tasks they have started, have frequent mood swings and a short temper, and often have a chronic pattern of underachievement. It is not surprising that many adults, after years of frustration with their academic, work, and social lives, have developed a low self-esteem. They often have a nagging sense of knowing something was wrong but never knowing exactly what it was. In many cases they have sought help with various mental health professionals who have overlooked ADHD and have never gotten to the bottom of what has been troubling them.

"Once they have been accurately diagnosed by a professional who understands ADHD, there is often a sense of tremendous relief at finally having an explanation for their long-standing difficulties. However, as with children, there is no 'cure' for adult ADHD. Therefore, learning how to cope with the manifestations of this disorder is critical to its effective management."

Endnotes

Chapter 3
1. Harvey C. Parker, *The ADD Hyperactivity Workbook,* (Plantation, Florida: Specialty Press, Inc., 1994), 107.

Chapter 14
1. Aphrodite Matsakis, *I Can't Get Over It - A Handbook for Trauma Survivors* (Oakland, CA: New Harbinger Publications, Inc., 1996), 16-17.

Chapter 15
1.   Stephen R. Covey, *The Seven Habits of Highly Effective People* (New York, New York: Fireside-Simon and Schuster, 1989), 81-85.

Chapter 18
1.   Daniel J. Wallace, *The Lupus Book - A Guide for Patients and Their Families* (New York, New York: Oxford University Press, Inc., 1995), 237.

Chapter 26
1.   American Psychiatric Association: *Diagnostic and Statistical Manual of Mental Disorders,* Fourth Edition (Washington, D C: American Psychiatric Association, 1994), xxi-xxii.

Chapter 27
1.   American Psychiatric Association: *Diagnostic and Statistical Manual of Mental Disorders,* Fourth Edition (Washington, D C: American Psychiatric Association, 1994), 78.

2.   Edna D. Copeland and Stephen C. Copps, *Medications for Attention Disorders (ADHD/ADD) and Related Medical Problems* (Plantation, Florida: Specialty Press, Inc., 1995), 86.